SCRIBNER REPRINT EDITIONS

*Jacques Maritain*

# ON
# THE PHILOSOPHY
# OF
# HISTORY

*EDITED BY JOSEPH W. EVANS*

AUGUSTUS M. KELLEY · PUBLISHERS
*CLIFTON 1973*

First Published 1957
(New York: Charles Scribner's Sons)
Copyright 1957 by Jacques Maritain

RE-ISSUED 1973 BY
AUGUSTUS M. KELLEY · PUBLISHERS
*Clifton New Jersey 07012*
*By Arrangement with* CHARLES SCRIBNER'S SONS

**Library of Congress Cataloging in Publication Data**

Maritain, Jacques, 1882-
On the philosophy of history.

(Scribner reprint editions)
1. History--Philosophy.   I.  Title.
D16.8.M286  1973            901            73-128059
ISBN 0-678-02760-9

PRINTED IN THE UNITED STATES OF AMERICA
*by* SENTRY PRESS, NEW YORK, N. Y. 10013

*To Reverend Father*
*Bernard I. Mullahy*
*with respect and gratitude*

# Table of Contents

vii

# *Foreword*

THE content of the present book is composed of four lectures which I gave in the course of a seminar at the University of Notre Dame in 1955, [and to which I later made a number of additions].

These lectures were recorded on tape; my friend Professor Joseph Evans was good enough to have them transcribed, and then to put them in readable form, trimming the text, inserting here and there answers or free developments which I had indulged in during the discussion, correcting the English style, and at the same time keeping the open conversational tone which is suitable here—in short, making a book emerge from an informal talk. It is a privilege for a philosopher to have his thought and intentions so perfectly understood. I wish to express my special gratitude to Professor Evans for the extreme care, thoughtfulness and devotion with which he has performed the work of editing. I also wish to tell him how pleased I am to have this book published in collaboration with him.

When Professor Evans sent me the four lectures for revision, I realized that, because of the limitations of time, I had omitted to make in them a certain number of points which I consider important. Thus my revision mostly consisted of writing new pages and affording, or so I hope, further elucidation.

Because of my distrust of Hegel, I was, in my youth, somewhat prejudiced against the very notion of the philosophy of history. Furthermore, as far as my own work is concerned, I have always shunned taking grand and imposing topics as sign-posts for my little essays. As a result, when in a remarkable and exceedingly generous article in the *Revue Thomiste*,[1] Msgr. Journet entered upon a study of *my* philosophy of history, I was quite surprised. At least he made me aware of the fact that I had made some incursions into the field, in a more or less scattered manner, according to the opportunities offered by the discussion of other problems. Msgr. Journet's article is an indispensable complement to the present volume. And it was of great assistance to me in the preparation of the lectures from which this book has issued. All the material I needed from my previous essays was collected and set in order there in a most helpful way. I am deeply indebted to Msgr. Journet, not only for this article, but also for the inspiration I received from his great book on the Church, and for his kindness in agreeing to read this book before publication, and to advise me about it.

I wish to express my warm thanks to Reverend Father Bernard I. Mullahy, Vice-Provincial of the Holy Cross Fathers,[2] without whose friendly prodding I would not have chosen this topic for my four lectures in 1955.

I regret that the pressure of time did not permit me to give more extensive developments to the present book, and, in particular, to make use, in my discussion, of the works of Herbert Butterfield, Isaiah Berlin, Christopher Dawson, and P. A. Sorokin, for whom I have special appreciation.

JACQUES MARITAIN

[1] Cf. Charles Journet, *D'une philosophie chrétienne de l'histoire et de la culture*, in "Jacques Maritain, son oeuvre philosophique," *Revue Thomiste*, Paris, Desclée De Brouwer, 1949.

[2] When he asked me to give these lectures he was head of the Department of Philosophy at the University of Notre Dame.

## Preliminary Note

In this book I shall make a tentative approach to the philosophy of history. I shall try to sum up many considerations and remarks which I have proposed on this subject over a number of years, and which are scattered in various books and essays.

The main subjects of my reflections will be as follows:

1) *the philosophy of history in general*, i.e., from the point of view of the theory of knowledge.

2) *axiomatic formulas or functional laws*—I mean those (more universal) formulas or statements which manifest the stability, in the course of history, of certain basic relations or fundamental characteristics.

3) *typological formulas or vectorial laws*—I mean those (more particularized) formulas or statements which deal with the very growth of history and the variety of its ages, phases, or aspects, and which manifest such or such typical direction in the historical development.

4) *God and history*, or rather: *God and the mystery of the world.*

*Chapter 1*

# THE PHILOSOPHY OF HISTORY
# IN GENERAL

We must first consider the philosophy of history from the point of view of the theory of knowledge. For many years the very notion of the philosophy of history was held in bad repute, because of Hegel, who was its putative father. (Before Hegel, however, there was Vico; and before Vico, St. Augustine . . . ) Hegel regarded himself as a kind of philosopher-God recreating not only human history but the whole universe. But as happens more often than not, error was the usher of truth in the human mind. Despite the errors of Hegel, and even, in a way, because of them—because of the way in which he was led to emphasize too strongly the aspect he had discovered in things—it is through Hegel that the philosophy of history was finally recognized as a philosophical discipline. And we are now called to a constructive task. The crucial problem to be tackled is: what can be a *genuine* philosophy of history?

## Is any Philosophy of History possible?

*1.* We have a first great example of such a philosophy in St. Augustine's *City of God*. Here we are given an interpretation of human history in the perspective of Christianity—an interpretation that opposed the oriental conceptions of the eternally recurrent phases of destruction and regeneration of the cosmos. Christianity has taught us that history has a direction, that it works in a determined direction. History is not an eternal return; it does not move in circles. Time is linear, not cyclical. This truth was a crucial acquisition for human thought.

St. Augustine's philosophy of history was a work of wisdom, both of theology and of philosophy, and more of theology. But in the mind of St. Augustine both wisdoms, the philosophical and the theological, worked together. And his *City of God* attempts to bring out the intelligible and, so to speak, trans-historical meaning of history, the intelligible meaning of the sequence or development of events in time. This is precisely the general object of the philosophy of history.

Yet we are immediately confronted with a preliminary objection: how can a philosophy of history be possible, since history is not a science? History deals only with the singular and the concrete, with the contingent,[1] whereas science deals with the universal and the neces-

---

[1] History deals with individual persons and individual events. Now it is true, of course, that once it has happened, an event cannot be changed, and that it has thus acquired a certain kind of necessity. But still this event as such was a contingent thing.

sary. History cannot afford us any explanation by universal *raisons d'être*. No doubt there are no "raw" facts; an historical fact presupposes and involves as many critical and discriminating judgments, and analytical recastings, as any other "fact" does; moreover, history does not look for an impossible "coincidence" with the past; it requires choice and sorting, it interprets the past and translates it into human language, it re-composes or re-constitutes sequences of events resulting from one another, and it cannot do so without the instrumentality of a great deal of abstraction. Yet history uses all this in order to link the singular with the singular; its *object* as such is individual or singular. The explanation given by an historian, as historian, is an explanation of the individual by the individual—by individual circumstances, motivations, or events. The historical elucidation, being individual, participates in the potential infinity of matter; it is never finished; it never has (insofar as it is elucidation) the certainty of science. It never provides us with a *raison d'être* drawn from what things *are* in their very essence (even if it be known only through signs, as in the sciences of phenomena).

What can we answer? I would answer that the fact that history is not a science does not make a philosophy of history impossible, because it is enough for philosophy itself to be "scientific"[2] knowledge and a formal or

---

[2] I am using here the words "science" and "scientific" in the broad Aristotelian sense (intellectually cogent or demonstratively established knowledge) which covers, in a quite analogical way, both *philosophy* and the *sciences* of phenomena.

systematized discipline of wisdom. And it is in no way necessary that the subject matter with which philosophy deals should be a subject matter previously known and worked out by some particular science. For instance, we have a philosophy of art, though art is not a science. The philosophy of art deals with the same subject matter as art, but it deals with it from the philosophical point of view and in a philosophical light. Therefore, we have a philosophy of art which is essentially distinct from art itself, and which provides us with philosophical knowledge about a matter which has not been previously scientifically elucidated. And I would make a similar observation if it were a question of the philosophy of nature. A philosophy of nature was possible before any developed scientific knowledge of nature, or when our scientific knowledge of nature was quite unsatisfactory. Thus it is that in the case of the philosophy of history we have a "scientific" object insofar as this object is the object of philosophy, but not insofar as the subject matter was previously scrutinized by some other scientific discipline.

I would say, therefore, that the philosophy of history has the same *subject matter* as history, which is not a science. And I might add, symmetrically, that the philosophy of nature has the same subject matter as physics and chemistry, which are sciences. But the philosophy of history has another *object* than history. It is concerned with an objective content—in Scholastic terms, a *formal object*—other than that of history and of the historical explanation; just as the philosophy of nature has a formal object other than that of physics and chemistry. In the case of the philosophy of nature, however, the formal object of physics and chemistry is scientific, and the formal object of the philosophy of nature is another intelligible and universal object, a more intelligible and a more universal object, in the sphere of the knowledge of nature. But in the case of the philosophy of history, the formal object of history is not scientific—it is not universal, not necessary, not raised to the level of abstract intelligibility. And the formal object of the philosophy of history is the only abstract and universal object, disclosing intelligible "quiddities" or *raisons d'être*, i.e., the only "scientific" (or rather wisdom-fitting) object, in the sphere of historical knowledge.

What philosophy needs as a basis, I may add, is the certitude of the facts, the general facts, from which it starts. Philosophy works on factual material which has been established with certainty. Now scientific facts are not the only well-ascertained facts. I remember Pierre Duhem, the celebrated physicist and historian of the sciences, insisting many years ago that the data of the senses or of common sense are in general more certain (they are less precise, and therefore they are not useful for science itself) than scientific facts. Therefore the data of the senses or of the common knowledge of man, when philosophically criticized, may serve as matter for the philosopher of nature. And similarly the data of history—I don't refer to the recitation of the details of singular events, which is but a presupposed background, but to certain significant general facts and factual relations—may serve as matter for the philosopher of history, because history is capable of factual certitude.

2. At this point we meet a problem which is preliminary to any discussion of the philosophy of history, namely, the problem of historical knowledge itself. What is the value of historical knowledge? Are there such things as historical truth and historical certitude? Dilthey was very much concerned with such problems. More recently Raymond Aron tackled the matter in two challenging essays[3] published before the second world war; as did Marc Bloch in his highly regarded *Apologie pour l'histoire*.[4] Today, more than ever, scholars are busy with the critique of historical knowledge, especially in France—I shall cite only Paul Ricoeur's and Henri Marrou's telling books.[5]

Henri Marrou is perfectly right in insisting that historical truth is utterly different from scientific truth, and does not have the same kind of objectivity. It is

---

[3] *Introduction à la philosophie de l'histoire; essai sur les limites de l'objectivité historique* (new ed., Paris, Gallimard, 1948). *Essai sur la théorie de l'histoire dans l'Allemagne contemporaine; la philosophie critique de l'histoire* (Paris, Vrin, 1938).

[4] Paris, Colin, 1949.

[5] Paul Ricoeur, *Histoire et vérité* (Paris, éd. du Seuil, 1955); Henri-Irénée Marrou, *De la connaissance historique* (Paris, ed. du Seuil, 1954). Cf. the review of the latter work by Charles Journet, *Nova et Vetera*, April-June 1955.

truth, or conformity with being, but the demonstration of which can *never* be finished (it involves an infinite); it has objectivity, but a peculiar sort of objectivity, in the attainment of which all of the thinking subject as an intellectual agent is engaged.

There is perhaps a little too much of Kantianism in Marrou's approach; but his thesis is, to my mind, fundamentally true. Since history is not concerned with abstract essences to be brought out from the singular, but with aspects of the singular itself to be picked up as particularly important, it is clear that the manner in which the historian directs his attention is a determinant factor in the process. And this direction of attention itself depends on the entire intellectual setting of the subject. So the entire intellectual disposition (I do not say, except in a most indirect and remote manner, the affective disposition, for the historian is not necessarily a poet, though perhaps the perfect historian would be a poet)—the entire *intellectual* disposition of the subject (the historian) plays an indispensable part in the attainment of historical truth: a situation which is totally at variance with scientific objectivity, where all that pertains to the subjective dispositions of man, except as regards the virtue of science, disappears or should disappear. For the historian it is a prerequisite that he have a sound philosophy of man, an integrated culture, an accurate appreciation of the human being's various activities and their comparative importance, a correct scale of moral, political, religious, technical and artistic values.

The value, I mean the *truth*, of the historical work will be in proportion to the human richness of the historian.[6] Such a position implies no subjectivism. There is *truth* in history. And each one of the components of the historian's intellectual disposition has its own specific *truth*. But the truth of history is factual, not rational truth; it can therefore be substantiated only through signs—after the fashion in which any individual and existential datum is to be checked; and though in many respects it can be known not only in a conjectural manner but with certainty,[7] it is neither knowable by way of demonstration properly speaking, nor communicable in a perfectly cogent manner, because, in the last analysis, the very truth of the historical work involves the whole truth which the historian as a man happens to possess; it presupposes true human wisdom in him; it is "a dependent variable of the truth of the philosophy which the historian has brought into play."[8]

[6] "Plus il sera intelligent, cultivé, riche d'expérience vécue, ouvert à toutes les valeurs de l'homme, plus il deviendra capable de retrouver de choses dans le passé, plus sa connaissance sera susceptible de richesse et de vérité." Henri Marrou, *op. cit.*, p. 238.

[7] This happens especially when the factual data and factual relations with which the historian is concerned are at an *optimum* of generality, neither too close to, nor too far from, the singular as such—just as for an object to be photographed there is an optimum distance not too close to, nor too far from, the camera.

[8] "Il n'y a pas d'histoire véritable qui soit indépendante d'une philosophie de l'homme et de la vie, à laquelle elle emprunte ses concepts fondamentaux, ses schémas d'explication, et d'abord les questions mêmes qu'au nom de sa conception de l'homme elle posera au passé. La vérité de l'histoire est fonction de la vérité de la philosophie mise en oeuvre par l'historien." Henri Marrou, *op. cit.*, p. 237.

3. Let us return now to the philosophy of history. Its objective content consists of universal objects of thought, which are either the typical features of a given historical age or some essential aspect of human history in general, and which are *inductively*[9] abstracted from historical data. It seems to me particularly important to stress the part played here by induction. A number of factual data are accumulated by history, and now from these data concerning a period of history or any other aspect of history some universal objects of thought are inductively abstracted by the philosopher. But in addition, these universal objects of thought must be *philosophically verified*, i.e., checked with some philosophical truths previously acquired. Then we see that they involve some intelligible necessity founded in the nature of things and providing us with a *raison d'être*. Induction and philosophical truths are and must be joined together in order to have the objective content of the philosophy of history.

I shall give but one example here. One of the axiomatic laws that I shall consider in Chapter II is the quite general and simple law according to which wheat and tares grow together in human history. It means that the advance of history is a double and antagonistic movement of ascent and descent. In other words, the advance of history is a two-fold simultaneous progress in good

[9] The way in which Toynbee (I shall have some critical remarks to make on his work in my concluding chapter) characterizes the great civilizations is a good example of the possibility of drawing through induction some typical characteristics relating to history.

and evil. This is a law of basic importance, it seems to me, if we are trying to interpret human history. Now such a law is first an inductive law drawn from observation, from a certain number of factual data about human history. But induction alone is not enough to constitute the formal object of the philosophy of history. It must be stabilized, so to speak, by philosophical reflection founded in human nature. In the present case, it is possible for the philosopher, once induction has warned and stimulated him, once it has attracted his attention to this fact of the double antagonistic movement—it is then possible for the philosopher to discover a root for this inductive fact in human nature. If we meditate on the simple notion of a rational animal, we find that progress toward good —*some* kind of progress toward good—is implied in the very concept of reason. Reason is by itself essentially progressive. Therefore, a being endowed with reason must necessarily, in some way or other, be progressive, not immutable, and progressive in the sense of progressing toward improvement, toward good. But, on the other hand, the notion of progress toward evil is implied in the essential weakness of a rational being which is an animal. If we think of this notion—a rational being which is not a pure spirit, but which is an animal, a being immersed in sensibility and having perpetually to make use of the senses and of passions and instincts—we see that such a being is necessarily weak in the very work and effort of reason. And this weakness will have more and more ways of manifesting itself as human possibilities increase. For all that, the law in question is not an *a priori* notion. My point is that neither induction alone nor philosophical deduction alone are sufficient. They must complement one another. I don't believe in a merely aprioristic philosophy of history, founded either on purely philosophical insights or on dialectical exigencies. But if we have these two lights together—the inductive light of facts and the rational light of philosophical analysis—both together fortify and strengthen one another. And both together constitute, in my opinion, the proper objective content of the philosophy of history, i.e., intelligible data and connections which have been drawn from facts by induction, but which are checked and verified by a rational analysis.

4. A further point has to do with the place of the philosophy of history in the whole realm of philosophy. Here I would like to recall a general principle in Thomist philosophy: it is *in* the singular, *in* the individual that science terminates. Not only does science begin with or start from the individual, but it terminates in the individual, completing therein the circle of its intelligible motion. This is why we have need of the senses, not only to draw from them our ideas of things, but also for the resolution of the judgment, which at least analogically must take place in the senses. As St. Thomas puts it, ". . . the judgment of the intellect is not dependent

on the senses in such a way that it would be accomplished through a sense organ, but rather it is dependent on them as on a final terminus with reference to which the resolution of the judgment takes place."[10] And again he writes: ". . . the end in which the knowledge of nature is achieved is above all (cf. Aristotle, *De Coelo*, III, 7) that which is perceived by the senses. Just as the cutler seeks the knowledge of the knife only in view of the work he has to do, or in order to make this particular knife, so the wise man seeks to know the nature of the stone or of the horse only in order that he may possess the reasons of the things which the senses are aware of." Note well Thomas' insistence on this final return to the senses, this final application of the abstract knowledge, with all the universal truths it grasps in things, to the particular known by the senses—this particular stone, this particular horse. "And as the judgment of the craftsman about the knife would be deficient if he did not know the work to be done, so the judgment of the wise man about the things of nature would be deficient if he did not know the objects of the senses,"[11] i.e., the singular attained by the senses.

Thus, we might say that some kind of return to the singular takes place at each degree of knowledge—not always in the same way, of course, but analogically, according to the various levels of knowledge. And I would

[10] *De Veritate*, XII, 3, ad 3. "Sicut extremo et ultimo, ad quod resolutio fiat. . . ."

[11] *Summa theol.*, I, 84, 8.

now suggest that a similar return to the singular must also take place with respect to philosophical knowledge as a whole. If this remark is true, we would have the philosophy of history as a kind of final application of philosophical knowledge to the singular, to that singular *par excellence* which is the course of human events and the development of history.

Let us illustrate this point in a diagram. We start from

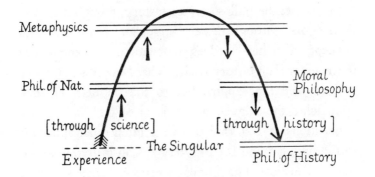

DIAGRAM NUMBER I

the level of experience, i.e., the level of the singular. Now the human mind ascends above this level toward various degrees of knowledge and abstraction. We have first the sciences, which look for rational regularity in the very world of experience but are not yet philosophy. At a higher level we have the philosophy of nature. And at the supreme level of natural wisdom, of philosophical wisdom, we have metaphysics. But I would stress that the curve is not finished—after ascending it descends, it has to come down. And here we have first moral philosophy, which depends on metaphysics but is much more concerned with the concrete and existential—the existential conduct of man. Then, in brackets, we have history, facing the sciences.[12] And finally, I propose, we have the philosophy of history as the final application of philosophical knowledge to the singular development of human events.

In a sense, the philosophy of history, though it knows the singular through more abstract and more universal concepts than history does, descends more deeply into the singular than history itself. What I mean is that there are two different approaches to the singular. History approaches the singular at the level of fact and factual connections. It is a kind of direct intellectual approach to the singular, and for this very reason it grapples with the inexhaustible. The singular is being besieged, squeezed more and more closely, by the particular concepts of the historian. And it always escapes our grasp insofar as it is singular.

I would add, parenthetically, that in the field of history, and precisely because history is not a science, a particular knowledge through connaturality is required

---

[12] I enclose history and the sciences in brackets to indicate that they are not part of the general philosophical movement represented in my diagram. I would merely point out that there is a certain symmetry or correspondence between history and the sciences, so far as they are both disciplines which are not philosophical.

of the historian—he must have some congeniality with the matter he is studying. For instance, he cannot really know military history if he has no experience of military things. Abstract knowledge is not enough[13]—he must have a real human experience of military things if he is to be able to interpret what happened in some particular case.

And I would say, finally, as regards this approach of history to the singular, that in history the singular is more deeply apprehended in a *factual* way than in the philosophy of history.

But with the philosophy of history we have a very different approach to the singular. Here we are at the level of abstract intelligibility and intelligible structures, and we have an indirect intellectual approach to the singular—to the singular, not in its singularity (that is why I call it indirect), but as a meeting point of general typical aspects which are to be found in a given individual, and which may help us to understand him. And by way of elucidating this remark, I would like to make a rapprochement between that discipline of wisdom which is the philosophy of history and such knowledge

---

[13] Charles Péguy engaged many years ago in a great controversy with the official historians at the Sorbonne. He reproached them, and I think quite rightly, for being *abstract* historians, considering history as a kind of accurate science. The pseudo-scientific history they were teaching at the Sorbonne was a fake, for history is not a science. And Péguy insisted that an historian must have an experiental knowledge, a knowledge through connaturality, of the matter in question.

as the classification of various types in quite humble "sciences" like physiognomy and graphology. The physiognomist and the graphologist have to do with something individual—the physiognomy or the handwriting of a person—but this something individual is analysed by way of general concepts, each one typical. And if a good physiognomist or a good graphologist is able to interpret the character or the psychology of a given person, it is by having recourse, not only to a process of intuitive mimicry, but also to general intelligible notions which have their focus in the individual in question but do not disclose him as such. In an abstract knowledge like the philosophy of history, the singular as such continues more than ever to escape. But the singular is more deeply apprehended in a *notional*, properly intellectual and expressible way, by means of all the various typical, general aspects which can be grasped in it.

To conclude now my remarks on the place of the philosophy of history in the body of philosophical disciplines, I would emphasize the fact, suggested in my diagram, that the philosophy of history is in connection with, and even belongs to, moral philosophy. It presupposes metaphysics and the philosophy of nature, of course, as does moral philosophy. But, like moral philosophy, it belongs in itself to practical rather than to theoretical philosophy, and this because of its existential character. And it is precisely because it is existential and practical that it presupposes the whole of philosophy—

practice presupposes theory, practical truth presupposes theoretical truth. Therefore the philosophy of history is connected with the whole of philosophy. And yet it itself belongs to practical and moral philosophy.

Indeed, the problem which must be faced with regard to moral philosophy, namely, whether moral philosophy is a merely philosophical knowledge, or a knowledge that must take into account theological data—this same problem (we will consider it later in this chapter) arises again, and in a much more pressing manner, with regard to the philosophy of history. To my mind, this is a sign that we have to do with the same type of discipline— moral philosophy. The philosophy of history is the final application of philosophical truths, not to the conduct of the individual man, but to the entire movement of humanity. And therefore it is *moral* philosophy.

To clarify still further its *practical* character, I would suggest that it is practical in the added sense that a really good statesman or man of action, even in the religious field, should be equipped with some genuine philosophy of history. The philosophy of history has an impact on our action. In my opinion, many mistakes we are now making in social and political life proceed from the fact that, while we have (let us hope) many true principles, we do not always know how to apply them intelligently. Applying them intelligently depends to a great extent on a genuine philosophy of history. If we are lacking this, we run a great risk of applying good principles wrongly—a misfortune, I would say, not only for us, but for our good principles as well. For instance, we run the risk of slavishly imitating the past, or of thinking, on the contrary, that everything in the past is finished and has to be done away with.

A final remark is that conjecture or hypothesis inevitably plays a great part in the philosophy of history. This knowledge is neither an absolute knowledge in the sense of Hegel nor a scientific knowledge in the sense of mathematics. But the fact that conjecture and hypothesis play a part in a discipline is not incompatible with the scientific character of this discipline. In biology or in psychology we have a considerable amount of conjecture, and nevertheless they are sciences. Why not in philosophy? Why could not philosophy have the privilege of conjecture and hypothesis? Why should it be condemned to deal only with absolute certainties? A discipline in which philosophical truths or certitudes are injected, so to speak, into induction, and fortify and strengthen induction, is all the more conjectural as the part of mere induction is greater in it. But it is not merely conjectural because, I repeat, it is never mere induction—there is always some rational necessity involved.

We cannot think of the philosophy of history as separated from philosophy in general. It deals with exemplifications of general truths established by philosophy, which it sees embodied in a most singular and

contingent manner. How could the certitudes of philosophy be manifested by historical reality if not in a more
or less conjectural manner? It is because the philosophy
of history is the final return of philosophical knowledge
to the individual and the contingent that it is absolutely
impossible for it to have (as Hegel foolishly believed)
the same degree of certitude as metaphysics. But nevertheless, by reason of its very continuity with the whole
body of philosophical knowledge, it is philosophy. It is
philosophy brought back to the most individual reality—
the movement, the very motion, of human history in
time.

## The Hegelian Delusion

5. I would now like to make a few remarks about what
I would call the Hegelian mirage or delusion. As I
observed at the beginning of this chapter, Hegel made
the place and importance of the philosophy of history
definitely recognized.[14] But, at the same time, he warped
and spoiled the philosophy of history in a pernicious way,
because of his effort to re-create history—as well as the
whole cosmos—as the self-movement through which
eternal Reason, that is to say God, actualizes Himself

[14] Not only is it now recognized, but we are in some respects poi-
soned by it. We have inherited from the nineteenth century the
most dogmatic, arbitrary and sophistic systems of philosophy of
history. But far from being a reason for despising and rejecting the
philosophy of history, this should stimulate us to try to discover
what is genuine and positive there.

in time (and finally reveals Himself in Hegelian wisdom). Everything had to be deduced from the various oppositions and conflicts of dialectics.

Nevertheless, the philosophy of history is, it seems to me, the *locus naturalis*—the natural place—of Hegel's central intuition, despite his insistence on logic. There was in Hegel, as in every great philosopher, a basic intuition which dealt with experience, with reality, and not simply with the *entia rationis* or reason-made entities of his dialectics. And this basic intuition has been described as the intuition of the mobility and disquiet which are essential to life, and especially to the being of man, who is never what he is and is always what he is not.[15] In other words, we might say that it is the intuition of *reality as history,* that is, as mobility, as motion, as change, perpetual change.

What caused Hegel to conceptualize this intuition in an erroneous system which is but grand sophistry was not only his idealism, but, above all, the way in which he decided to carry rationalism to the absolute, and make human reason equal to divine reason, by transforming dialectics into "absolute knowledge" and absorbing the irrational in reason,—hence the dialectical self-motion, which is both the very life and the revelation of reality. The fact remains, nevertheless, that in the very world

---

[15] Cf. Jean Hyppolite, *Genèse et structure de la phénoménologie de l'esprit* (Paris: Aubier, 1946), pp. 143-145, and his reference to H. Marcuse, *Hegels Ontologie und die Grundlegung einer Theorie der Geschichtlichkeit* (Frankfurt, 1932).

of extra-notional being, history as such, which like time completes its being only by memory and the mind, offers for our consideration the development of dynamic ideas or intentional charges which are at work in collective consciousness and are embodied in time. These historical ideas—forms immanent in time, so to speak—presuppose nature, the being of things and the being of man, and they have nothing to do with the Hegelian Idea and the self-engendering processes of Hegel's onto-logic. In addition, these historical ideas are very far from constituting the whole of history. Admittedly, if we consider the manner in which these historical ideas are at play in history, it can be said that each one of them, each one of these forms immanent in time, can reach its final accomplishment in time only by provoking its opposite, and denying itself. But why is this so? It is because its very triumph exhausts the potentialities which summoned it, and at the same stroke unmasks and provokes in the abyss of the real the opposite potentialities. Here is an interpretation which has nothing to do with the dialectical alienation and reintegration, but which shows, it seems to me, that history offered Hegel a kind of material which was akin to his general philosophy.

But this particular play of ideas in history is only one of the aspects of history. History discloses to us its intelligible meaning through many other aspects and many other laws that are more important still and closer to reality. As I mentioned above, Hegel refused to see that the philosophy of history is an inductive discipline, in which the analysis of the empirical concrete and philosophical knowledge enlighten one another. In reality, he was himself guided by experience and he used induction.[16] It could not have been otherwise. But he did not confess the importance of the role played in his own thought by experience and induction. He tried to mask all this, to have it appear as a mere illustration of a logical *a priori* necessity which he had discovered by merely logical means. And he did this because he was busy re-engendering the whole of reality, and explaining history as the necessary development of Reason itself, and the "true theodicy."

Great irrationalist though he may have been, Hegel, as we previously observed, carried modern rationalism to its peak. He made philosophy into the absolutely supreme wisdom. And yet Hegelian philosophy was not merely philosophical. Hegel's philosophy tried to swallow up all the theological heritage of mankind by recasting it in merely rational terms. His was an effort to digest and assimilate in philosophy all the religious and theological, indeed all the spiritual problems of humanity. In the last analysis, the Hegelian metaphysics and the

[16] There are even many valuable inductive insights in Hegel's work, such as, for instance, so far as the philosophy of history is concerned, the notion of the "beautiful individuality" which he uses to characterize Greek civilization. Another—quite obvious—example of inductive generalization is his linking of the Roman world and the notion of right. Another—more original—is his characterization of the Roman Emperor (*Herr der Welt*).

Hegelian philosophy of history are modern gnosticism —they are pure gnosticism. Trying to re-engender the whole of reality by means of dialectics, he engulfed the world of experience in logical entities—*entia rationis*— in mutual conflict, which composed for him an immense polymorphous and moving idol, as vast as the world, whose name was first Nature, and then History, when man emerges from nature, and when the anthropo-theistic process of self-realization is thus revealed.

6. It may be added that the Marxist notion of history derived directly from Hegel, with a transformation from idealism to materialism. With both Hegel and Marx it was substantially the same notion, the same idol: because, in the last analysis, Marxist dialectics is Hegelian dialectics, shifted from the world of the Idea to the world of matter. This Hegelian derivation is the only explanation of the very expression "dialectical materialism." Matter itself, for Marxism, is inhabited and moved by logical movement, by dialectical movement. In other words, in Hegelian idealism we have *entia rationis*— those of the logician or dialectician—haunted by reality, by experiential knowledge forcefully introduced into them; whereas in Marxism we have reality or matter[17] haunted by *entia rationis*.

---

[17] The Marxist theorists confuse these two notions. When they speak of materialism they are often thinking of realism, and when they speak of realism they are often thinking of materialism.

Marx's and Engels' matter in self-motion, and their historical materialism, are only by-products of Hegelian dialectics put (as Engels said) on its feet instead of on its head. It is exactly the same dialectics, but with its feet now, thanks to Marx, on the ground instead of in the air. And the Marxist philosophy of history is but Hegel's very philosophy of history which has grown atheistic (instead of pantheistic and anthropo-theistic) and which makes history advance toward the divinization of man thanks to the dialectical movement of matter.

7. I would like to conclude these observations on Hegel with a few words about human freedom in history. With respect to the supra-individual entities engendered by the movement of the Idea, Hegel entirely relativized the individual person. The human person is for him but a wave which passes on the ocean of history, and which fancies that it pushes the flood while it is carried on by it. And all the greatness of the great figures of history is to have entered the exigencies of time, to have perceived what time had made ripe for development. In *King Lear* Edgar says: "ripeness is all." It is so for Hegel —ripeness is all. The great man in human history only grasps or understands more or less obscurely what is ripe for development, and then works to carry into existence this fruit already prepared by history. Thus, Hegel explains, and quite intelligently, how the genius of history—the cunning of Reason—uses the interests

and passions, even the most egoistic passions, of great
men of history: they are in reality the puppets of the
*Weltgeist,* of the spirit of the world. And never does
Hegel speak of their conscience, of the part played by
their reason, by their freedom, by what is most genuinely
human and rational in them.

To put things in a more general light, let us say that
Hegel disregards human freedom to the very extent to
which he does not see that the *mode* in which an historical change necessary in itself is brought about depends on this freedom. Given a certain period or age
in human history, there are certain changes which are
necessary in themselves, or with respect to the cumula-
tive needs they answer. But this is not because of a kind
of divine dialectics, the dialectics of Hegel. Rather, it is
because, given the structure and circumstances of human
history, certain things become impossible—the human
being can no longer live in such or such conditions;
some change must occur in a given direction. There are
some changes in human history which are necessary. But
to say this is not enough, because the *manner* or *mode*
in which these changes occur is *not* necessary: it depends
on human will and human freedom. In other words, the
necessary change in question can be brought about in
one way or in another—ways quite different as to their
spiritual or rational meaning. Take, for instance, the
implications of scientific, industrial and technological
progress. It is obvious that the passing of humanity

under a technological regime is something necessary; it cannot be avoided. But in what spirit, in what manner? In such a way that man is made subservient to the machine and to technique, or in such a way that technique and technology are made instruments of human freedom? The same change can come about in an enslaving and degrading manner, or in a genuinely rational and liberating manner. And that does not depend on any necessity in history, but on the way in which man intervenes, especially great men, great figures in history.[18]

Hegel disregarded the reality of this impact of human free initiative on human history. The same can be said of Marx, though he made greater than Hegel did the role of the will and energies, especially the collective will and energies, of man. Marx insists that men make their own history, but they do not make it freely, under conditions of their own choice; they make it under conditions directly bequeathed by the past. Well, such a formula can have two interpretations—either the Marxist interpretation or the Christian interpretation.

[18] Pierre Vendryès expresses well this basic notion that there are in human history necessary trends and that at the same time there is no inevitability: "Jamais les engrenages de l'histoire n'ont un caractère fatal. Les cycles n'ont pas une évolution déterminée. Chacun d'eux peut se trouver ouvert ou fermé. . . . Tout en étant entraînés par elle, les hommes font leur histoire. Entre les événements il reste toujours quelque intervalle libre dans lequel la volonté humaine puisse développer ses propres chances." De la probabilité en histoire (Paris, Editions Albin Michel, 1952), p. 299. See also two important studies: Isaiah Berlin, Historical Inevitability (London and New York, Oxford University Press, 1954), and Pieter Geyl, Debates with Historians (Groningen, Holland, J. B. Wolters, 1955).

For Marx it meant that the freedom of man is but the spontaneity of a vital energy which, by becoming conscious of the movement of history, is made into a most efficacious force in history. The revolutionary thinker is like a prophet and titan of history, insofar as he reveals history to itself, discovers the pre-ordained direction of its movement (what was ripe for development), and guides in this pre-ordained direction the effort of human wills. But there is no exercise of human free choice, and no capacity in man for modifying and orienting the movement of history in a measure which may appear quite restricted in comparison with the whole of history, but which is crucial in relation to the fate of the human persons themselves and of generations to come.

For a Thomist, on the contrary, this same formula— man makes history and history makes man—would mean that history has a direction, determined with regard to certain fundamental characteristics by the immense dynamic mass of the past pushing it forward, but undetermined with regard to specific orientations and with regard to the spirit or the manner in which a change, necessary in other respects, will be carried into existence. Man is endowed with a freedom by means of which, as a person, he can, with more or less difficulty, but really, triumph over the necessity in his heart. Without, for all that, being able to bend history arbitrarily according to his desire or fancy, man can cause new currents to surge up in history, currents which will struggle and compound with pre-existent currents, forces and conditions so as to bring to final determination the specific orientation, which is not fixed in advance by evolution, of a given period of history. If, in fact, human freedom plays in the history of the world a part which seems all the greater as the level of activity considered is more spiritual, and all the smaller as the level of activity considered is more temporal, this is because man, collectively taken, lives little of the properly human life of reason and freedom. It is not surprising, in view of this fact, that he should be "in submission to the stars" in a very large measure. He can, nevertheless, escape from them, even in his collective temporal life. And if we consider things from a sufficiently long perspective of centuries, it seems that one of the deepest trends of human history is precisely to escape more and more from fate. But here again we meet with the law of the double and antagonistic motion of ascent and descent together. Thus, the development of our material techniques seems, on the one hand, to make historical fate weigh more heavily on man; and, on the other hand, this same development offers man unexpected means of freedom and emancipation. In the end, which of these two aspects will be predominant depends on the free will and the free choice of man.

## Spurious and genuine Philosophy of History

*8.* The Hegelian system is the most brilliant, telling, and powerful form, but it is far from being the only form of spurious philosophy of history.

Good historians—because they have personal experience of the contingencies, complexities, and uncertainties of historical work, nay more, of the element of relative non-intelligibility that is involved in history—have a natural distrust for the philosophy of history. This natural distrust becomes an all-too-justified loathing when they are confronted with the spurious philosophy of history which is, as a rule, to be found on the market.

What is it that makes them angry and unhappy when they concern themselves with the notion of a philosophy of history? They are incensed by the intolerable dogmatism of philosophies which pretend to be rational disciplines and which (whether they claim, with Hegel, to save religion by making it a mythical chrysalis of their own "absolute knowledge" or, with Marx, to sweep away religion in the name of the good tidings of atheism or, with Auguste Comte, to build up a new and definitive religion, the religion of Humanity) offer themselves to mankind as the messengers of some messianic revelation, and use history as an instrument to validate their empty claims.

Furthermore, the historians (for instance, Henri Marrou in his book mentioned above) reproach the philosophy of history with four capital sins: first, its almost inevitably oversimplified, arbitrary and wanton approach in regard to the choice of materials, the historical value of which is assumed for the sake of the cause; secondly, its self-deceptive ambition to get at an *a priori* explanation of the course of human history; thirdly, its self-deceptive ambition to get at an *all-inclusive* explanation of the meaning of human history; and fourthly, its self-deceptive ambition to get at a so-called *scientific* explanation of history, the word "scientific" being used here in this quite peculiar sense, which can be traced back to the sciences of nature, that with such an explanation our thought enjoys a kind of intellectual mastery over the subject-matter.

And yet, the historians of whom I am speaking cannot help recognizing that, once the problem "does the pilgrimage of mankind, triumphant and heart-rending by turns, through the duration of its history, have a value, a fecundity, a meaning?" has been posed, it cannot be eluded.[19]

What do all the previous observations point to? They tell us that the historian cannot help feeling the appeal of the philosophy of history, and that at the same time he thinks he must resist this appeal, given the spurious forms in which, as a rule, the philosophy of history greets

[19] Cf. Henri Marrou, *op. cit.*, p. 16.

his eyes. What he is loathing in reality is not genuine philosophy of history, but the *gnosticism of history*— that gnosticism of history which was carried by Hegel to supreme metaphysical heights, but which is to be found also, at quite another level, in a system as completely fascinated by positive sciences and as decidedly anti-metaphysical as Comte's system is.

*9*. Spurious philosophy of history, thus, is gnosticism of history in the most general sense of this expression, and insofar as it is characterized by the four "capital sins" that have just been mentioned.

Contrariwise, a genuine philosophy of history, to which we pointed in the first section of this chapter, does not claim to dismantle the cogs and gear-wheels of human history so as to see how it works and master it intellectually. History, for it, is not a problem to be solved, but a mystery to be looked at: a mystery which is in some way supra-intelligible (insofar as it depends on the purposes of God) and in some way infra-intelligible (insofar as it involves matter and contingency, and depends on the nothingness injected into it by man when he does evil). The question, therefore, is only to perceive in such inexhaustible subject-matter certain intelligible aspects, which will always remain partial and somehow disconnected. Theology does not *explain* the divine Trinity. Analogically, the philosophy of history does not *explain* history. And so, any temptation to the first afore-mentioned "capital sin" is reduced for it to a minimum, and it is immune to the three others, for the simple reason that a genuine philosophy of history does not dream of being an explanation of history. And where there is no explanation, there can be neither *a priori* explanation, nor all-inclusive explanation, nor master explanation.

Let us, then, state as our first principle: history can be neither rationally *explained*[20] nor *reconstructed* according to necessitating laws.[21]

But history can be *characterized, interpreted* or *deciphered in a certain measure and as to certain general aspects*—to the extent to which we succeed in disclosing in it meanings or intelligible directions, and laws which enlighten events, without necessitating them.

*10.* I have emphasized in another book[22] this basic truth that the laws of nature are necessary but that the course of events in nature is contingent. The necessity proper to *laws* does not make the *events* necessary, because the laws refer, in one way or another, to universal essences brought out from things by abstraction, while the events take place in existential, concrete, individual reality, which lies open to the mutual interference of

[20] As against all philosophies of history of the Hegelian or dialectical type.

[21] As against all philosophies of history of the Comtian or supposedly "scientific" type.

[22] Cf. *The Degrees of Knowledge* (New York: Scribners; London: Bles), Chapter II.

independent lines of causation, and which is made of nature and adventure.

If this is true in the realm of nature, it is still more true in the realm of history, because in the course of the events of nature we have to do only with contingency, whereas in the course of the events of history we have to do also with the free will of man. The observations I have submitted above on human freedom and history presupposed a certain metaphysics, which sees the problem of free will as a central problem to be thoroughly sifted, and which considers the existence of free will an essential characteristic of man. But the philosophy of history of Hegel, of Marx, or of Comte (not to speak of their persistence in confusing "necessary laws" with "necessitating laws") presupposes either a certain metaphysics or a certain anti-metaphysics which dreams of going beyond the alternative: freedom or determinism, and, as a result, disregards or ignores in practice the reality of free will in man. Hence, the awkward and silly way in which, while they depict—explain or reconstruct—human history as a self-development resulting, in each of its phases, from the inflexible requirements of necessitating laws, either dialectical or phenomenal, they try at the same time to make room for "human freedom" (in a most equivocal sense), human initiative and human energies in the shaping of events. Auguste Comte had at least the merit of frankly exposing such a self-contradictory position, when he prided himself on his bastard concept of *fatalité modifiable*, "modifiable inevitability."

At this point we have to make clear that no philosophy of history can be genuine if the general philosophy it presupposes, and of which it is a part, does not recognize the existence of human free will (together with the other properties of the human person) and the existence of God: the consequence of these two truths being that human history implies a double kind of contingency, on the one hand with respect to the transcendent freedom of God, and on the other hand with respect to human free will as well as to natural accidents and vicissitudes.

If we do not believe in the existence of human free will, we cannot understand how man can exert, as I mentioned above, a decisive influence on the mode or specific orientation of an historical change which is necessary in itself, or with regard to the accumulated needs it answers; and we cannot realize, either, that the historical necessity in question refers to a kind of general pattern which is, as a rule, undetermined and, so to speak, neutral with respect to what matters most to the hearts of men: whereas the mode, specific orientation or specific inspiration which depends on human freedom has to do with what has, for good or ill, the most direct impact on human persons and human societies.

And if we do not believe in the existence of God, we shall not, of course, see history as governed by Him from above, and as continually modeled and remodeled by His eternal purposes, making up for the evil through which human free will spoils human history, and turning losses into greater gains. But then, if we do not look at history as at a tale told by an idiot, and if we try to work out a philosophy of history, we shall, in our effort to make history rational, transfer to it the very rationality which no longer belongs to transcendent divine purposes; in other words, we shall transform these formerly divine purposes either into history's own inner purposes and dialectical requirements, or into "scientific" laws which shape its development with sheer necessity. It was the misfortune of the philosophy of history to have been *advertised* in the modern world by philosophers who were either the greatest falsifier in divinity, or utter atheists. Only a spurious philosophy of history could be elicited by them.

*11.* Let us conclude this section with a few words about the structure of time.

The subject-matter of the philosophy of history is the unrolling of time, the very succession of time. Here we are confronted not only with the singularity of particular events, but with the singularity of the entire course of events. It is a story which is never repeated; it is unique. And the formal object of the philosophy of history is the intelligible meaning, as far as it can be perceived, of the unrolling, of the evolution in question.

Now I would merely observe that time, the time of human history, has an inner structure. Time is not simply a garbage can in which practical men would have to pick up more or less profitable opportunities. Time has a meaning and a direction. Human history is made up of periods each of which is possessed of a particular intelligible structure, and therefore of basic particular requirements. These periods are what I have proposed calling the various historical climates or historical constellations in human history. They express given intelligible structures, both as concerns the social, political and juridical dominant characteristics, and as concerns the moral and ideological dominant characteristics, in the temporal life of the human community. The typological laws in the philosophy of history, which I mentioned in my Preliminary Note, have to do with these various historical climates. I shall consider them in Chapter III.

With the question of the structure of time, which I just touched upon, the question of its irreversibility (or of its not cyclical, but "linear" or "vectorial" character) is closely connected. In this regard, I would like to bring to our attention some significant observations made by Mircea Eliade. In his book, *Le mythe de l'éternel retour*,[23] he stresses the fact that the *acceptance* of time—and of history—far from being matter-of-course for man, is for him a difficult and dearly paid achievement. Man is naturally frightened by the irreversibility of his own duration and the very newness of unpredictable events.

[23] Paris, Gallimard, 1949. (Eng. tr.: *The Myth of the Eternal Return*, Bollingen Series, Pantheon Books, 1954).

He refuses to face them. Hence the negation of time by archaic civilizations. They defended themselves against the dire reality of history either by constructing mythical archetypes, or by assuming a periodic abolishment and regeneration of time, and a periodic recurrence of the same historical cycles. As I pointed out at the beginning of this chapter, acceptance of time and of history was a conquest of Christianity and modern times. But this very acceptance would be of a nature to drive man to despair if he could not decipher some transhistorical meaning in the awful advance of time into the night of the unknown, thronged with perpetually new perils.

### Philosophy of History and Moral Philosophy adequately taken

*12.* Once more, the philosophy of history is no part of metaphysics, as Hegel believed. It pertains to moral philosophy, for it has to do with human actions considered in the evolution of mankind. And here we have either to accept or to reject the data of Judeo-Christian revelation. If we accept them, we shall have to distinguish between two orders—the order of nature and the order of grace; and between two existential realms, distinct but not separate—the world, on the one hand, and the Kingdom of God, the Church, on the other. Hence, we shall have to distinguish between a theology of history and a philosophy of history. There is a theology of history, which is centered on the Kingdom of God and the history of salvation—a theology of the history of salvation[24]—and which considers both the development of the world and the development of the Church, but from the point of view of the development of the Church. And there is a philosophy of history, which is centered on the world and the history of civilizations, and which considers both the development of the Church and the development of the world, but from the point of view of the development of the world. In other words, the theology of history is centered on the mystery of the Church, while considering its relation to the world; whereas the philosophy of history is centered on the mystery of the world, while considering its relation to the Church, to the Kingdom of God in a state of pilgrimage.

If this is true, it means that the philosophy of history pertains to moral philosophy adequately taken, that is to say to moral philosophy complemented by data which the philosopher borrows from theology, and which deal with the existential condition of that very human being whose actions and conduct are the object of moral philosophy. The moral philosopher must take into account all data (even if they depend on some kind of supra-rational knowledge) which contribute to make the *real* man, the

[24] See Charles Journet's *Introduction à la théologie* (Paris: Desclée De Brouwer, 1947), pp. 73-76; 159-203.

existential condition of man, genuinely known to us.[25] A moral philosophy and a philosophy of history conceived in the perspective of Judaism, or Moslemism, or Hinduism will not be faultless—they are, however, sure to be less basically deficient than any moral philosophy or philosophy of history which is supposedly merely rational and philosophical. The integrity of the concrete perspective in which such disciplines perceive human things depends on the truth-value of the religious tradition with which they are connected. As a result, believing, as we do, that the Christian perspective is the completely true one, we may say that the wisdom of history—what Berdyaev called "historiosophy"—is the business of Christian theology, but it is also the business of Christian moral philosophy.

And I would suggest that Christian moral philosophy is more disposed than theology to feel the proper importance of time and the temporal order. It is more disposed

[25] See my books *An Essay on Christian Philosophy* (New York: Philosophical Library, 1955) and *Science and Wisdom* (London: Bles; New York: Scribners, 1940). In my view, this use or consideration of the data of theology must take place in moral philosophy because moral philosophy has to do with a practical object, the conduct of man. Therefore, it needs to know the existential condition of man in its integrity; it needs to know not only human nature but also original sin, grace, etc. But when it comes to speculative philosophy, to metaphysics, for instance, there is no need of such a dependence on theological data, because here we have only to consider the natural content of reality. It is another question whether speculative philosophy needs, for its completion, to be guided by faith, protected by the truths of faith. In its own realm it does not have to borrow anything from theology.

to see that they have their own finalities and their own created values, even though they are means in relation to eternity. Christian philosophy is concerned with the direction of human history, not only in relation to the work of eternal salvation, on which history has an impact, but also and primarily in relation to that very work accomplished in human history which is in itself terrestrial and immanent in time.

But what about the pure philosopher—the philosopher who recognizes only the light of natural reason, who refuses any data deriving from theology concerning the existential condition of man? In his hands the philosophy of history is bound either to fail in its own expectations, or to risk mystification, for in order to get at some level of real depth and significance it inevitably requires prophetic data. And where would the pure philosopher find authentic prophetic data? It seems to me that the philosophy of history is an outstanding example of the necessity for a true philosophy of man, an integrally valid moral philosophy, to have the philosopher illumine the knowledge of the natural order with the light of a more elevated knowledge received from theology, while he uses the method proper to philosophy and advances with steps, so to speak, of philosophy, not of theology.

As a confirmation of these views, let me refer to two books written by distinguished scholars whose perspectives are more or less different from mine (very different in the second case), and whose convergence with my own conclusions is all the more interesting to me.

I am thinking, in the first instance, of Josef Pieper's book: *Über das Ende der Zeit, eine geschichtsphiloso-phische Meditation.*[26] Pieper, to my mind, makes the whole *opus philosophicum* too dependent on theology. But, and this is what matters most for me, he insists that no philosophy of history is possible without the illumina-tion of theology, for, as he puts it, the essential question for the philosopher who contemplates history is: what is the end of history? "A question which deals with the sal-vation and doom of man. . . ."

In the second instance, I am thinking of Mircea Eliade's afore-mentioned book, especially its chapter "La terreur de l'histoire." It is Eliade's contention that "the horizon of archetypes and repetition cannot be transcended with impunity unless we accept a philosophy of freedom that does not exclude God. And indeed this proved to be true when the horizon of archetypes and repetition was trans-cended, for the first time, by Judaeo-Christianism, which introduced a new category into religious experience: the category of *faith*."[27] And he goes on to say that faith, in the sense in which he uses this word—the faith which moves mountains—implying for man the highest con-ceivable freedom, the freedom to step into the very fabric of the universe, means "a new formula for man's

[26] *The End of Time* (London: Faber and Faber; New York: Pan-theon, 1954).

[27] *Op. cit.,* pp. 236-237. (Eng. tr., p. 160).

collaboration with the creation," the only one which "(aside from its soteriological, hence, in the strict sense, its religious value) is able to defend modern man from the terror of history—a freedom, that is, which has its source and finds its guarantee and support in God." In other words, Christianity is the vital perspective proper to "the *modern* man" and to "the *historical* man," that man "who simultaneously discovered personal freedom and continuous time (in place of cyclical time). . . ." And it alone can give us "the *certainty* that historical tragedies have a transhistorical meaning, even if that meaning is not always visible for humanity in its present condition."[28]

Clearly, the consequence of such considerations is that the proper climate for the development of a genuine philosophy of history is the intellectual climate of the Judaeo-Christian tradition.

[28] *Ibid.*, pp. 238-239. (Eng. tr., pp. 161-162).

## Chapter 2

# AXIOMATIC FORMULAS
# OR FUNCTIONAL LAWS

These formulas or laws deal with any part of the historical development or with the whole of it. They express a functional relation between certain intelligible characteristics, certain universal objects of thought—a functional relation which exists, and which can be verified in one way or another, at each step of the development of human history.

### The law of two-fold contrasting progress

*1.* I mentioned in Chapter I the law that history progresses both in the direction of good and in the direction of evil. By way of elucidating this further, we might meditate on a famous parable in the Gospel. Of course, the Gospel is not concerned with the philosophy of history, but we do find in it the most illuminating statements for the philosopher of history—statements which we may use from our own philosophical point of view, in applying them to this particular matter, the philosophy of history. I am thinking of the parable in Chapter XIII of the Gospel according to St. Matthew about the man who sowed good seed in his field, only to have his enemy come and oversow it with cockle:

> The kingdom of heaven is likened to a man that sowed good seed in his field.
>
> But while men were asleep, his enemy came and oversowed cockle among the wheat and went his way.
>
> And when the blade was sprung up and had brought forth fruit, then appeared also the cockle.
>
> And the servants of the goodman of the house coming said to him: Sir, didst thou not sow good seed in thy field? whence then hath it cockle?
>
> And he said to them: An enemy hath done this. And the servants said to him: Wilt thou that we go and gather it up?
>
> And he said: No, lest perhaps gathering up the cockle, you root up the wheat also together with it.
>
> Suffer both to grow until the harvest, and in the time of the harvest, I will say to the reapers: Gather up first the cockle and bind it into bundles to burn, but the wheat gather ye into my barn.

This parable is a quite striking expression of the law we are now considering. It means that good is not divided from evil in human history—they grow together. Let us first consider its primordial, its religious meaning. Its proper object is the kingdom of grace; it refers to the ultimate end beyond the world. The evil works accumulated in time will burn in hell, and the good works accumulated will be gathered into the divine barn. But pending the end, sinners and saints will grow together. Thus, from the point of view of the history of the kingdom of grace, or of Christ's mystical body, it may be said that two immanent movements cross each other at each point of the evolution of mankind, and affect each of its momentary complexes. One of these movements draws upward (toward final salvation) everything in mankind that participates in the divine life of the kingdom of grace, or the Church (which is *in* the world but not *of* the world), and follows the attraction of Christ, Head of the human race. The other movement draws downward (toward final doom) everything in mankind which belongs to the Prince of this world, head (as St. Thomas says)[1] of all evildoers. It is in undergoing these two internal movements that human history advances in time. The Christian knows that, though constantly thwarted and constantly concealed, the work of the spirit is carried out in spite of everything, as history goes on, and that thus from fall to fall, but also from obscure gain to obscure gain, time marches toward the resurrection.

A particular instance of this double movement is pointed out by St. Thomas when he is considering the state of mankind during the time between the original sin and the coming of Christ.[2] Briefly, St. Thomas says

[1] *Summa theol.*, III, 8, 7.
[2] See *Ibid.*, III, 61, 3, ad 2.

that with the development of time sin began to make its impact felt more and more in the human race in such a way that the instinct of natural law became insufficient for man to act rightly, and it thus became necessary to have the precepts of written law. In this increase of the weight of sin we have the movement downward. But we have simultaneously the movement upward: there is the divine gift of the Decalogue; there are the sacraments of the Ancient Law; and there is the progressive increase in the knowledge of divine things; through the teaching of the prophets the elements of faith are disclosed bit by bit—until the full revelation achieved by Christ. This instance of the double movement concerns, of course, the kingdom of grace and the ultimate end beyond the world.

2. But what I would like to emphasize particularly now is that the parable of the wheat and the cockle has a universal meaning and bearing which is valid for the world as well as for the kingdom of grace. And we must say, from the philosophical point of view, that the movement of progression of societies in time depends on this law of the double movement—which might be called, in this instance, the law of the degradation, on the one hand, and the revitalization, on the other, of the energy of history, or of the mass of human activity on which the movement of history depends. While the wear and tear of time and the passivity of matter naturally dissipate and degrade the things of this world and the energy of his-

tory, the creative forces which are proper to the spirit and to liberty and which are their proof, and which normally have their point of application in the effort of the few, constantly revitalize the quality of this energy. Thus the life of human societies advances and progresses at the cost of many losses. It advances and progresses thanks to the vitalization or superelevation of the energy of history springing from the spirit and from human freedom. But, at the same time, this same energy of history is degraded and dissipated by reason of the passivity of matter. Moreover, what is spiritual is, to this very extent, above time and exempt from aging.

And, of course, in certain periods of history what prevails and is predominant is the movement of degradation, in other periods it is the movement of progress. My point is that both exist at the same time, *to one degree or another*.

We have here a notion of progress which is quite different both from the necessary, rectilinear and indefinite progress which the eighteenth century dreamed of, and in which future things were supposed to be always and by right better than past ones; and, on the other hand, from that negation of any progress and that disregard for the God-given élan at work in us which prevail among those who despair of man and of freedom.

The deeper our knowledge of anthropology becomes, the more, I think, shall we become aware of the fact that the most telling instance of the law I am discussing took place in the ages when mankind passed from its childhood to its adult state. No progress upward was more important than this coming of human thought and human societies to rational knowledge (as contradistinguished from mythical knowledge) and to political life (as contradistinguished from tribal life). Yet the simultaneous downward movement cannot be overlooked. The concept of the *good savage*, as cherished by the eighteenth century, was a silly notion of over-civilized people; there was no more *innocence*, absolutely speaking, in the primitive man than in the child each one of us was. The fact remains, nevertheless, that there was *a kind* of innocence in both. There were in the myths of primitive man an obscure grasping of essential truths—in his approach to things a power of imaginative intuitivity and a vital participation in nature—in his tribal life a real and probably heartening, though slavish, communion with the group, which have been lost in the process.

Shall we look for another instance? Let us think of a few striking features of modern history. On the one hand we have, from the last decades of the eighteenth century on, an awareness of human rights and of the dignity of the human person, a longing for freedom and human fellowship, a recognition of the principle: government of the people, for the people and by the people, a growing concern for civil liberties and for social justice, an assertion of man's power over nature which constitute an exceptionally significant progress upward. But, on the other hand, we are confronted, during the same space of time, with the subjection of all citizens to military service, with more and more destructive wars, with the growth of mercantile materialism, then of nationalist passions, then of communism, of fascism, of racism, and, in those years which will always be alive in our memory, with the mass murder of six million Jews by Hitler; the first half of the nineteenth century witnessed the enslaved conditions of life to which the industrial proletariat was then submitted; and our own times face the threat to human freedom raised by communist totalitarianism thriving in large regions of the earth.

May I now allude to the problem of the temporal mission of the Christian? As I indicated in Chapter I, the philosophy of history has practical consequences, which shows that it pertains to the domain of practical or moral philosophy. From the genuine notion of progress, which I just emphasized, a practical consequence can be drawn with respect to the work of the Christian in the world. The work of the Christian in history does not aim to set the world up in a state from which all evil and all injustice would have disappeared. If it did, then it would be only too easy, considering human history, to condemn the Christian as a utopian, or to say, as some Protestant theologians do, that, given the corruption of human nature, the very notion of a Christian (that is, Christian-inspired) civilization, and of an effort to make Christian justice and brotherhood prevail in the world, is a contradiction in terms.[3] The work of the Christian is to maintain and augment in the world the internal tension and the movement of slow deliverance which are due to the invisible potencies of truth and justice and love, in action in the mass which goes counter to them. And this work cannot be in vain—it surely produces its fruit. We have no illusions about the misery of human nature. But we have no illusions, either, about the blindness of the pseudo-realists who cultivate and exalt evil in order to fight against evil, and who consider the Gospel a decorative myth which we could not take seriously without throwing the machinery of the world out of order.

Genuine Christianity does not forget the original greatness of man. It abhors the pessimism of inertia. It is pessimistic in the sense that it knows that the creature comes from nothingness, and that everything that comes from nothingness tends of itself toward nothingness. But its optimism is incomparably more profound than its pessimism, because it knows that the creature comes from God, and that everything that comes from God tends toward God.

[3] I remember a discussion I once had with an eloquent and dynamic Protestant theologian, who was also a Socialist deputy of the French Parliament. "If you are so hopeless about any Christian possibility in the world," I asked him, "why, then, are you a Socialist? Do you not hope for some improvement in terrestrial justice?" And he answered: "I am a Socialist, a Protestant Socialist, only to *protest* against evil and injustice. But I don't hope for any truly Christian accomplishment in the terrestrial order, I don't believe that any Christian civilization will ever be possible."

3. To conclude my remarks on the law of the double antagonistic movement, I would observe that we find a particular application of this law in what might be called the law of the parasitical part played by error in the progress of human speculative or theoretical knowledge, especially in the realm of our knowledge of nature and in the realm of philosophy. What I mean is that great discoveries are usually paid for in human history by the reinforcement that a given truth receives from error preying upon it, and from the emotional overtones that error provides. For instance, the mathematical knowledge of nature—that great scientific conquest which started in the sixteenth and seventeenth centuries—was stimulated and fortified by a mistaken philosophy (the mecanist philosophy) which preyed upon it and appeared for a long time as inseparable from it. And we may think that without the ambitions developed by mecanist philosophers the human mind would not have been sufficiently enflamed to make the progress that was this discovery of mathematical knowledge of nature. Similarly, we might say that the awareness of science as a knowledge of phenomena, distinct from philosophy, that is, from knowledge of intelligible being, took place at the same time as Kantian philosophy. It is, so to speak, thanks to the errors of Kant that this notion of science (our modern science) as knowledge of phenomena was recognized in human history. Also, we might say that the great psychological discoveries about the unconscious were reinforced

and stimulated by the erroneous philosophy of life which prevailed in the mind of Freud.

### The ambivalence of history

4. This law is a consequence of the law of the double movement. If human history is subject to the two contrasting movements noted above, then we may say that at each moment human history offers to us two faces. One of these faces gives grounds to the pessimist, who would like to condemn this period of history. And the other gives grounds to the optimist, who would like to see the same period as merely glorious. Thus, there were many in the nineteenth century—among them such prophets as Victor Hugo—who confused the past with darkness and error, and regarded the future as all light and goodness. This condemnation of the past was a foolish mistake in the philosophy of history. But in the same century there were many Christians who condemned modern times as pure and simple aberration. And this was equally a foolish mistake. No period of human history can be either absolutely condemned or absolutely approved. It is as irrational to condemn the Middle Ages, from the rationalist point of view, as to condemn modern times, from a so-called Christian point of view.

There were, to be sure, great spiritual errors in modern times: but great truths were also discovered, which deal with the order of nature and natural reason, and are of importance for the spirit. The Rousseauist errors which, especially in Europe, preyed upon the democratic principle, and the false philosophies with which it was often confused by accident, and which are corroding it from within, ask for a purification of this principle; but they also ask for a deeper recognition of its intrinsic truth, as well as of its vital connection with Gospel inspiration. The hope of mankind as to its temporal life is inseparably tied up with the advent of democratic philosophy in modern times.

An error in spiritual principle bears its inevitable fruit: we must expose the error and avow the loss. During the same period, however, there is an advance in human affairs, there are new human conquests. There are, joined to certain evils, gains and achievements that have an almost sacred value since they are produced in the order of divine Providence: we must acknowledge these achievements and these gains.

The ambivalence of history can be seen in the development of the Roman Empire; or in the post-Constantine mutual embrace between Church and State; or in the various phases of the industrial revolution; or in the present reign of physico-mathematical science and of technology. . . . Today a most obvious example of this ambivalence is offered to us by the advent of the atomic age, with its inherent capacities for the destruction of mankind as well as for an unheard-of improvement of its life.

5. It is in a Christian perspective that I have, for a long time, brooded over my reflections on the philosophy of history. Let me, then, speak in this perspective. St. Gregory wrote: "Men should know that the will of Satan is always unrighteous but that his power is never unjust," for "the iniquities he proposes to commit God allows in all justice."[4] This saying goes a long way. It supplies an important principle of historical exegesis.

The devil hangs like a vampire on the side of history. History goes on, nonetheless, and goes on with the vampire. It is only in the kingdom of grace, in the divinely assisted life of the Church, that the devil has no place. He plays his part in the march of the world, and in a sense spurs it. Is he not eager for the better insofar as in his view the better, as a French saying puts it, "is the enemy of the good"? He does not scruple, on occasion, to court the better in order to destroy some good, not to improve it. And thus he happens to do in his particular way, which is a wrong way, and with perverse intention, what good people omit to do because they are asleep. That which is done is done badly, but it is done. There is a passage full of strange meaning in the hymn of Habacuc (as translated in the Vulgate). It is said there that the devil goes before the feet of God: *et egredietur diabolus ante pedes ejus.*[5] He runs before Him. With vicious (and ultimately defeated) purpose, he prepares His ways—as a traitor.

[4] *Moralium, lib.* II, cap. 10, n. 16, P. L., LXXV, 564.
[5] Habacuc, 8, 5.

Manichaeism is no better philosophy of history than relativism. People who deify human reason are almost inevitably driven to a sort of Manichaean conception of history which Christian thought avoids. When the prime good, when the first and fundamental measure by which all else is measured, is something in the human order, this good will have an opposite; and this opposite, being opposed to the supreme good, can only have the office of pure evil. If the absolute good is political liberty, or political order, there will be in history elements of pure darkness, either the "tyranny" that is opposed to this liberty, or the "utopian dreams" that are opposed to this order. If the primary good is Cartesian thinking, there will be ages and philosophies assigned to utter darkness of which the progress of thought can hope for no good result. It is the old struggle of Ormuzd against Ahriman, the old Manichaean struggle.

The Christian knows that God has no opposite Absolute; there is no opposite prime principle.[6] For the Christian there is indeed a struggle between light and darkness, between truth and error. But there cannot be for him in existing reality *pure* darkness or *pure* error, because all that is, in the measure in which it is, is of God, and is good. In the thought of the atheist or, if you will, of the "enemy of God," as Proudhon called himself, it is impossible that God be at the service of the enemy of God; whereas in the thought of the Christian the enemy of God is at the service of God. God has His adversaries,

---

[6] Cf. *Summa theol.*, I, 49, 3.

not in the metaphysical but in the moral order. Yet His adversaries are always, finally, at His own service. He is served by the martyrs, and He is served by the executioners who made the martyrs.

Everything that happens in the history of the world serves in one way or another the progress of the kingdom of grace and (sometimes at the price of a greater evil) some kind of progress in the world. Voltaire, while setting out to run down the Church and make fun of religious faith, was nevertheless in Christendom and in the history of Christendom as he was in the created universe and in the order of Providence. He served them in spite of himself. He fought for an error in his campaign for tolerance, since he thought of "dogmatic" tolerance, as if freedom of thought were an absolute end without any law higher than subjective opinion;[7] yet this campaign caused him at the same time to fight against another error, namely the modern error, which has found expression in the formula *"cujus regio ejus religio,"* that the force of the State and social pressure have of their own nature a right to control conscience. In this respect, Voltaire was striving without knowing it for Article 1351 of the Code of Canon Law—"No one shall be compelled to embrace the Catholic faith against his will." He was instrumental in making modern societies recognize the principle of civil tolerance.

I find a symbol of the truths to which I just alluded

[7] On the distinction between "dogmatic tolerance" and "civil tolerance," see my book *Man and the State*, pp. 180-182.

in G. K. Chesterton's invaluable book, *The Man Who Was Thursday:* there we are shown the police and the anarchists—who fight each other conscientiously—obedient to the same mysterious lord whom the author calls Mr. Sunday....

6. Another remark can be made relating to the diverse perspectives or points of view which are peculiar to the speculative theologian, the theologian of history, and the philosopher of history. What about their respective attitudes when they come to deal with an event like schism or heresy in religious history?

The speculative theologian will look for the truth of the matter. He will be busy with analyzing and refuting the errors involved, clarifying and enlarging in this connection the horizons of truth. The schism or the heresy in question will be considered in its intrinsic meaning and abstract essence.

The theologian of history will observe that in the course of time, and despite the permanent impulse of such communities toward separation, a greater and greater number of those who are brought up in the religious communities involved are made, by reason of their good faith, exempt from the sin of schism or heresy, so that these religious communities should not be called "heretical" or "schismatic," but simply "dissident."[8]

The philosopher of history will be mainly concerned

[8] Cf. Charles Journet, *L'Eglise du Verbe Incarné*, t. II, pp. 708-799.

with the effects and repercussions of the spiritual events in question on the history of the world and of civilization. And then he will be confronted, on the one hand, with direct destructive results (say, for instance, the way in which the Lutheran rupture ruined the precarious unity of Europe and shut Germany up in her own national dreams and frustrations). But, on the other hand, he will also be confronted with indirect creative repercussions: it was, for instance, in the historical situation resulting from the very state of religious division engendered by Protestantism that in actual fact the great political achievement brought about by America took place—I mean a Constitution and a civil society which are religiously inspired and cling to the Judaeo-Christian tradition, and which at the same time fundamentally oppose any discrimination among citizens by reason of their religious denomination.[9]

Finally it is not irrelevant to say a few words, no longer about the Manichaean temptation, but about quite another temptation, in full swing today, the Hegelian and Marxian temptation, which makes a number of our contemporaries subservient worshippers of history. They think that the only evil is to resist history; the only doom, to be rejected and repudiated by history. History has become for them the Saviour and Redeemer. The primary moral obligation, then, is to keep pace with history—and

[9] Cf. Peter F. Drucker, "Organized Religion and the American Creed," in *The Review of Politics*, July, 1956.

to have historical efficacy and to succeed in history. The one who does not succeed in history is condemned, and justly condemned—he has sinned against history.

Someone who, as we have seen, plays his part in history enjoys the show and laughs at them. Those who make it their first principle to advance with history, or to make history advance and to march in step with it, thereby bind themselves to collaborate with all the agents of history; they find themselves in very mixed company.

We are not co-operators with history; we are co-operators with God.

No doubt, to absent oneself from history is to seek death. Spiritual activity, which is above time, does not vacate time, it holds it from on high. Our duty is to act on history to the limit of our power: yes, but God being first served. And we must neither complain nor feel guilty if history often works against us: it will not vanquish our God, and escape His purposes, either of mercy or of justice. The chief thing, from the point of view of existence in history, is not to succeed; success never endures. Rather, it is *to have been there*, to have been *present*, and that is ineffaceable.

### The law of the historical fructifications of good and evil

7. This law deals with the relation between ethics and politics. I have discussed it at some length in an essay

entitled "The End of Machiavellianism."[10] Here I will merely sum up some of my observations in this essay.

I would recall, in particular, that the good in which the justice of human societies bears fruit, and the misfortune in which the injustice of human societies bears fruit, "have nothing to do with the immediate and visible results; historic *duration* must be taken into account; the temporal good in which the state's justice bears fruit, the temporal evil in which its iniquity bears fruit, may be and are in fact quite different from the immediate results which the human mind might have expected and which human eyes contemplate. It is as difficult to disentangle these remote causations as to tell at a river's mouth which waters come from which glaciers and which tributaries. The achievements of the great Machiavellianists seem durable to us, because our scale of duration-measurements is an exceedingly small one, with regard to the time proper to nations and human communities. We do not understand the fair play of God, Who gives those who have freely chosen injustice the time to exhaust the benefits of it and the fullness of its energies. When disaster comes to these victors the eyes of the righteous who cried against them to God will have long putrefied under the earth, and men will not know the distant source of the catastrophe."[11] Let it be noted parenthetically that when

[10] See *The Review of Politics*, January, 1942; also my book *The Range of Reason* (New York: Charles Scribner's Sons, 1952), pp. 134-164.
[11] *Ibid.*, pp. 149-150.

these lines were written, Hitler and Mussolini were win-
ning on all scoring boards. . . .

On the other hand, it must be made clear that human
communities, nations, cities, civilizations—all of which are
collective wholes incapable of immortality—and which
by essence are at the same time moral and physical, depend on physical conditions. Good or bad, they can, like
Atlantis, be victims of a tidal wave. This means that
justice and moral virtues do not abolish the natural laws
of aging of human societies; they do not hinder physical
catastrophe from destroying them. What must be said,
consequently, is that justice and rectitude (and this is the
law I wish to emphasize) *tend in themselves* to the preser-
vation of human societies and to a real success in the
long run; and that injustice and evil *tend in themselves*
(leaving aside what concerns physical conditions) to the
destruction of societies and to a real failure in the long
run.

I would like to quote, at this point, a few lines of
Chateaubriand which are inspired by genuine political
and historical wisdom, and which appear to me as sin-
gularly up to date. Speaking of Danton and the French
Revolution, and alluding in passing to the judgment and
death sentence of Charles the First, "Danton," he said,
"more candid than the English, said: 'We will not try
the king, we will kill him.' He also said: 'These priests
and nobles are not guilty, but they must die, because they
are out of place, they hinder the movement of things

and get in the way of the future.' These words, which may seem so horribly profound, have nothing of genius in them: because they assume that innocence is nothing, and that the moral order may be cut off from the political order without causing the latter to perish, which is false."[12]

### *The law of the world-significance of history-making events*

*8.* I was somewhat at a loss for the proper words to express the law I have in mind. In fact, I am still searching for the proper expression of a truth which I think I perceive, but which seems to me to be rather difficult correctly to formulate. My main difficulty has to do with the notion of the "unity of the world" or "unity of mankind" and its true meaning. We have, it seems to me, a hint that there is some sort of formless and structureless unity of the world as a whole, and that every human community, people or nation, at every point on the earth, is affected, be it in a most remote way, by what happens to the other human groups. There is in the world, however, nothing akin to the spiritual unity of the Church, and we must take care not to think of things which belong to the natural order in terms of theological concepts like that of the "communion of saints." I

[12] Translated from *Mémoires d'outre-tombe* (Garnier edition), Vol. II, p. 20.

should like to be able to delineate the possible rational meaning of the mysterious unity of the world as a whole; I am sorry I did not arrive at any satisfactory formulation, though, given the modern network of economic, intellectual and political communications, encompassing all peoples, such a concept, so far as it is equivalent to that of universal interrelation, may obviously be translated into quite rational terms. Yet I was thinking of a more vital and secret kind of solidarity, as old as mankind is. . . .

Under these circumstances, and pending further elucidation, I shall say "the world" only in a restricted sense, using this word as synonymous with a given ensemble of peoples in which, different as they may be, a certain community in spiritual and cultural background, and in historical experience, hope, and suffering has been at work for a sufficiently long time.

Well, what I have in mind is that the world (at least in the sense I just indicated) has a kind of vital unity—not political, not organized, not manifested, but real nevertheless. And by reason of this vital unity, when a history-making event, a big event for mankind, an event which carries to actuality century-old potentialities and aspirations, occurs at a particular point in space, say, in a given nation or a given people, it does not occur only for this nation or this people, but it occurs *for the world*. It is not only an event or a change for this particular nation or this particular people; it is an event or a change for the world—I mean, of course, with most diverse, contrasting and opposite effects. It has happened for the world, though it will affect the other parts of the world in ways quite different from the way in which it has taken shape at its point of origin. And at the same time it has exhausted, so to speak, the quantity, the amount of creative energy which was required for its occurrence in human history. It has no longer any significance for the making of history; it is already in the past.

Let us think, for instance, of the French Revolution. Looking at the previous centuries—especially the times of the baroque age, the absolute monarchy, and the social order, founded on inequality, peculiar to the *Ancien Régime*—we see that a creative change, a history-making change had become necessary. When it took place, with all the human hopes it carried in itself and the stains it was soiled with, it took place in France. Yet it happened not only for France, but for the world as well. Those parts of Europe which escaped it in its inborn and typical, revolutionary French forms, and which fought it with the greatest energy, had nevertheless their own way of digesting its historical content, and adapting, for better or worse, their own structures and traditions to the new phase of history. On the whole, the attack of the brass and the counter-attack of the strings were but one theme in the concerto. At the same time, the creative historical energy which had brought about the French Revolution was exhausted. Both historical creativity and historical necessity shifted to other changes in preparation.

*9.* Not to speak of their intrinsic features, there is, from the point of view of our present considerations, a basic difference between the French Revolution and the Russian Communist Revolution. Spoiled as the French Revolution may have been with Rousseauist philosophy, Jacobinism, the crimes of the Terror, and the hatred and persecution of the Church, the true principles and the message of Liberty, Equality, Fraternity that it conveyed asserted themselves for their own sake, independently (as to their very essence) of the vicious trends which preyed upon them. Contrariwise, the elements of truth contained in the Soviet Revolution are inseparably engaged in a false and totally dogmatic system of the world which rivets them to error, and does not even permit them to assert themselves in the open (thus it is that the very notion of social justice has no recognized status in the ideology of dialectical materialism). Only if the system breaks into pieces can these elements of truth be set free.

Now my point is that, the basic difference in question being taken into account, the historical law we are discussing is also to be verified in the case of the Russian Communist Revolution. If we consider the sequence of previous centuries, we realize that some history-making change was necessary in the social order. We have only to remember the fortune of the word "revolution" in Europe before the First World War—everybody was speaking of revolution. And Charles Péguy, who was an old Proudhonian revolutionary, said that the social revolution would be ethical or it would not be at all—"la révolution sociale sera morale ou ne sera pas." Now it *was*, it occurred; and it was *not* ethical. But suppose that at that time, before the First World War, there had been in Europe a Christian Gandhi, a man equipped with a more complete social philosophy than Gandhi's but possessing Gandhi's spiritual energy, and capable of grouping together the forces of the most active parts of the working classes. Then the historically necessary change of which I am speaking could have occurred in the form of a Christian social revolution. From an abstract and theoretical point of view, it is a possibility that instead of Marx we might have had another thinker and social leader, of Christian persuasion, criticize the forms of the industrial civilization of his day, and set out to change them, in the name of justice, freedom, and love, not of hatred and social war, and the myth of the deification of man through the messianic advent of the proletariat.

As a matter of fact, the revolution in question occurred in the form of a Marxist atheist revolution in a given part of the world, in Russia. There the revolution took place, and it was an internally corrupted revolution—not Péguy's ethical revolution, but the dialectical-materialist revolution of Lenin. The history-making event was intrinsically rotten; yet it had happened, and it had happened not only for Russia, but for the world. I mean that the possibility of having now a Péguyistic, if I may put it so, a Christian social revolution take place—this possibility was blotted out. It is too late. The act of the historical drama has been performed; we are now at another step in history. What Christians have to do is not to dream now of a Christian social revolution, but to endeavor to make the Christian ideal prevail in the gradual adjustments through which a non-Communist world (whose social structure and life, at least in the United States, is already beyond capitalism and beyond socialism) will bring about the changes required by that social justice which the Communist revolution was forbidden by its own ideology even to mention—though the yearning for it among the masses was the real incentive it traded upon.

On the other hand, it is clear that the Communist revolution can expand in some other parts of the world, as it did in China. But such a change, serious as it may be, can only have the meaning and value of a local change—not of a change "for the world." And the Communist revolution cannot win the world, not only because of the resistance of the non-Communist nations, aware of the danger and determined to check it, but also because this revolution has no longer any possibility of bringing about, in any given spot in the world, a break in universal history, a history-making change. The Communist agitators are now men of the past. Their effort to upset Western civilization and to introduce the Communist regime into it is but an effort to subject it to what is in reality a past event, a dead event, in human history. It is a vital necessity for freedom-loving peoples to fight and block this effort. Yet in so doing they are not struggling with a threatening novelty, but with a threatening past. There was much wisdom in the old Chinese fear of the dead. Corpses may be pernicious enemies. For all that, they lack the breath of life. The Communist revolution has lost its historic steam. It is to new problems and new changes to come that the creative energy of history has shifted, thus rendering necessary new history-making events. And it is the job of human free will to prepare and bring about these events in the right direction and under an inspiration really worthy of man.[13]

---

[13] For example, the effort toward a supra-national unity of the world pertains to the order of new problems and new changes. But the question of how to achieve a supra-national unity, a world government, can be solved in a quite tyrannical direction, issuing in some kind of super-Empire, or in a truly pluralist and freedom-loving manner. (See my book, *Man and the State*, Chapter VII.)

Another new problem and new change, particularly crucial and urgent for present times, relates to the political emancipation of the peoples which were subjugated—and at the same time carried along into the stream of universal history—by the colonial regime. Here is an historic revolution which in order to foster, not sheer violence and irreconcilable hatreds, but at last a sufficient dose of mutual understanding and cooperation for the common good of mankind, requires not only that amount of generosity which is inseparable from political intelligence, but also the effort, inspired

## The law of prise de conscience

*10.* This is the law of growth in awareness as a sign of human progress, and as involving at the same time inherent dangers. I think that this law of progressive *prise de conscience* is linked with the history of civilization in general, but it takes place very slowly. And while it takes place in one area, another area may be completely immune to it. In Greece, for instance, there was an awareness of the political freedom of the citizen, but not of the spiritual inner freedom of the human person with respect to the city. For the Greek conception of the city was a kind of "hieropolitical" conception, disregarding the emergence of what is eternal in man above the temporal community. In philosophy, the awareness of the theory of knowledge as a particular discipline came very late. Of course, Aristotle and all great philosophers had a theory of knowledge. But it was necessary to wait for Kant to have the theory of knowledge built up into a special theory, a special discipline. And this was a progress in the structure of the body of philosophical disciplines.

---

by fraternal love, of Christians aware of their temporal mission. And we know that such an effort is being made.

Adolf Berle's *Tides of Crisis* (New York: Reynal, 1957) appeared while I was correcting my own proofs. I can only mention it. I would have liked to quote from the chapter "Battle of the Past Against the Future" and from what the author says, in a general way, of the historical "ghosts" and their "armies of conscripts" in this remarkable book.

### The law of the hierarchy of means

*11.* We really have two laws here. The first is the law of the *superiority of humble temporal means ("moyens pauvres") over rich temporal means, with respect to spiritual ends.* We may describe as *rich* temporal means those which, implicated in the density of matter, of their own nature postulate a certain degree of tangible, visible success. Such means are the peculiar means of the world. It would be absurd to despise or reject them; they are necessary; they are part of the natural stuff of life. Religion must consent to receive their assistance. But it is proper for the health of the world that the hierarchy of means be safeguarded in their proper relative proportions.

There are other temporal means, which are the peculiar means of the spirit. They are *humble*[14] temporal means. The Cross is in them. The less burdened they are by matter, the more destitute, the less visible—the more efficacious they are. They are the peculiar means of wisdom, for wisdom is not dumb; it cries in the market-place, it is its peculiarity so to cry, and hence it must have means of making itself heard. But the mistake is to think that the best means for wisdom will be the most

---

[14] I have said in French *"moyens temporels pauvres."* It is very difficult to translate this expression accurately into English. If we say *"poor* temporal means," I am afraid it is just the contrary of what I mean. "Humble" is a good enough word, I think, but unfortunately it leaves aside the notion of poverty, which is quite important here.

materially powerful means, the biggest and the most expensively equipped as to mass-communication and propaganda.

The pure essence of the spiritual is to be found in wholly immanent activity, in contemplation, whose peculiar efficacy in touching the heart of God disturbs no single atom on earth. The closer one gets to the pure essence of the spiritual, the lighter and less palpable, the more spontaneously tapering become the temporal means employed in its service. And that is the condition of their efficacy. Too tenuous to be stopped by any obstacle, they pierce where the most powerful equipment is powerless to pierce. *Propter suam munditiam.* Because of their purity they traverse the world from end to end. Not being ordered to tangible success, involving in their essence no internal need of temporal success, they participate, for the spiritual results to be secured, in the efficacy of the spirit.

*12.* The second law having to do with the hierarchy of means may be called the law of the *superiority of spiritual means of temporal activity and welfare over carnal means of temporal activity and welfare.* Here it is a question of means with respect to a temporal work, not to a spiritual end—let us say, to a social or political work which has, for the sake of the highest interests of man, justice, freedom, peace, fraternal love, to overcome prejudice or egoism, greedy ambition or oppressive

power. And let it be added, that which bore witness to
the law I have in mind was more often than not the self-
sacrifice of magnanimous men who were also forgotten
men. In other words, the law in question was at work in
human history in a particularly humble and hidden way,
more or less in the manner of a ferment—never in the
foreground, except as regards a few shining examples in
our century.

Here I think it is relevant to examine the example and
the testimony of Gandhi. In my opinion, this testimony
is particularly significant for Christians. As a matter of
fact, Gandhi was inspired both by the Indian Scriptures
and by the Gospel—he read the Gospel a great deal. His
originality was to set apart the means of patience and
voluntary suffering and to organize them systematically
into a particular technique of political action. Now we
might relate this technique to the Thomistic notion that
the principal act of the virtue of fortitude is not the act
of attacking, but that of enduring, bearing, suffering with
constancy. A Thomist would elucidate what Gandhi
called non-violence by the notion of the means pertaining to courage in enduring. And the question would be
to apply these particular means to a temporal end to be
achieved.[15]

Gandhi himself was convinced that these means can be
applied in the West as they have been in the East. To my
mind, whether they follow the method of Gandhi or

[15] See my *Du régime temporel et de la liberté* (Paris: Desclée De
Brouwer, 1933), Annex II.

some method yet to be invented, men who are fighting in the temporal field and who attach importance to spiritual values, especially those who struggle for the advent of a Christian-inspired civilization, are likely to be led willy-nilly to a solution along these lines. It seems to me to be significant that this new awareness of the power of the means of love and of spiritual means in the temporal order took place in our century at the same time as the power of the state developed, and even was contemporary with the appearance of the totalitarian states. Once again, it is always the same law of dual, contrasting motion—a development in one direction, and another development, which compensates for the first one, in another direction. We are now waiting for the manifestation of the full dimensions of Christian temporal activity.

I would now remark (and this seems to me particularly important from the point of view of the philosophy of history) that Gandhi was not only an exceptionally great and prophetic figure. He should be considered the founder of a school of thought. He left disciples. I am thinking especially of Vinoba, who now has a tremendous influence in India. There is, thus, a continuity in this use of spiritual means tending to some temporal transformation. Vinoba was successful in obtaining from land-owners considerable changes in the division and distribution of lands to poor farmers. He is a real continuer of Gandhi.[16]

[16] See, for instance, Lanza del Vasto, *Vinoba ou le nouveau pèlerinage* (Paris: Denoël, 1954). Also, Hallam Tennyson, *India's Walking Saint, Vinoba Bhave* (New York: Doubleday, 1955).

To conclude, the question I am merely posing is whether some kind of similar activitiy can develop in the Western world. Up to now we have very few signs of it. But what may appear impossible now can become possible in a future less distant perhaps than we imagine. I do know that there are now in France a few people (and people of real intellectual stature) who have started, with some friends abroad, a common effort in fast and prayer either to obtain, in such or such a given case, more justice from governmental policies, or to bring about more mutual understanding and peaceful cooperation between various groups, such as the Moslem, Jewish and Christian groups; the initiator is Louis Massignon. In Sicily there is the collective non-violent struggle led by Danilo Dolci. A few sporadic attempts to put Gandhian methods into application are also appearing here and there in this country; and particular importance must be attached in this connection to the great example given by the Negroes of Montgomery and Reverend Martin Luther King, their religious leader.[17] This is not the place

[17] We read in the *New York Times*, December 10, 1956:

"Montgomery, Ala., Dec. 9 (AP)—About 3000 Negroes closed today a week-long institute on nonviolence and social change. It marked the first anniversary of the Montgomery bus boycott.

"The Rev. Martin Luther King Jr., president of the Montgomery Improvement Association, which has led the boycott and sponsored the institute, told the group that 'we have had a glorious week here together.'

"The week included seminars on the way that Montgomery's 50,000 Negroes have conducted the boycott. The passive resistance used in protest against city bus segregation was described as an

to discuss the specific purposes which are being pursued in these various instances. The thing I am interested in is the fact of their existence, and their historical meaning. Such beginnings are very small, almost imperceptible. Their prospective significance is, I believe, not small.

---

example to Negroes elsewhere in their battle against racial discrimination.

"The United States Supreme Court decided Nov. 13 that interstate bus segregation was unconstitutional and ordered it ended in Montgomery. The city and the state of Alabama have asked for a rehearing."

## Chapter 3

# TYPOLOGICAL FORMULAS
# OR VECTORIAL LAWS

*1.* These formulas or laws manifest the variety of ages or aspects in human history. They relate to what may be called *vectors of history*—I mean given segments determined in extent and direction and in significance. They relate also to the relationship between one vector and another, given a certain perspective or line of consideration.

I would suggest that the inductive process has a still greater part to play in this kind of law than in the axiomatic laws. One of our examples will be the distinction to be made between the *magical* and the *rational* states or regimes of human thought and culture. Here induction appears preponderant. Given the data of anthropology, we are confronted with the inductive fact that there is some big difference between the way of thinking of primitive man and our own way of thinking (so much so that the primitive man's way of thinking was first described as "*pre-logical* mentality").[1] But we cannot

[1] Lucien Lévy-Bruhl, who coined this expression (I was a student of his at the Sorbonne, and I always liked this scrupulously sincere and fair-minded positivist), first seemed to hold the intellect of the

rest on this purely inductive notion. Furthermore, it must be re-elaborated, re-stated, if it is to be correctly conceptualized. For this we have to call upon some philosophical notions or insights—for instance, the knowledge of certain "natures" like imagination and intellect, and the knowledge of their relationship and connection in the progress of human knowing. A certain universal idea will then emerge, grouping and giving account of the various characteristics of primitive mentality and civilized mentality—what I call *imagination-ruled regime or state*, on the one hand, and *intellect-ruled regime or state*, on the other. And given this notion, which is not a simple induction but rather a rational insight quickening induction, we perceive that there is a certain internal necessity for a historic transition from one state to the other.

### The theological notion of the various "states" of human nature

2. Let us first turn our attention to data which have nothing to do with induction, because they are theological data, but which are particularly illuminating and suggestive for the philosopher of history, because they provide him with a basic framework and basic indications

---

primitive man and its laws of functioning as different in *nature* from our civilized intellect. Later on he came to other conclusions and accepted the interpretation founded on the notion of *state*.

about the direction of human history. This is in keeping with, and indeed a particular instance of, the significance these data have for the moral philosopher.

I have in mind the theological notions of the "state of pure nature," the "state of innocence or integrity," the "state of fallen nature," and the "state of redeemed nature." As we know, according to Catholic theology the state of pure nature never existed—it is a mere possibility; and the state of fallen nature and the state of redeemed nature are to be distinguished, but they are not in succession—because God never abandoned fallen nature to itself, divine grace never ceased being at work in mankind; in other words, fallen nature was to be redeemed either by virtue of Christ's passion *to come* or by virtue of Christ's passion *already come*. Now I would simply propose here a few remarks on two questions suggested by this theological distinction of the states of human nature.

A first question is: can the fact of the original fall of man be proved, demonstrated by reason, brought out by some inductive process? It seems that Pascal would answer in the affirmative. He seems to have thought that given the contradiction, on which he insisted so much, offered by human nature—unheard-of misery, on the one hand, unheard-of grandeur, on the other—there must have been in the human past some catastrophe which will account for this contradiction. And therefore the original fall would appear to him as rationally proved by the analysis of human nature in the condition in which it can be observed by us.

I do not believe that it is possible to prove such a thing. It depends on a revealed datum; it does not pertain to the philosophical realm. The original sin, however, did not only deprive human nature of the supernatural gifts proper to the state of adamic innocence; it also *wounded* human nature. That is a theological datum on which St. Thomas lays particular stress. And these wounds of our nature are a reality always present in the human race. Hence, it appears that if the fact of the Fall cannot be demonstratively inferred, nevertheless there should be signs—for instance the very ones emphasized by Pascal —which cause reason to conclude in a *probable* manner that such an event took place at the dawn of our history. Here we have a problem which is of great import for moral philosophy and the philosophy of history in their own fields.

I have no intention of discussing it here (though, in my opinion, the question should be answered in the affirmative). I would prefer to submit a few remarks connected with the problem.

We might first observe that what we experientially know of man has to do with the real and concrete man, man in the state of fallen and redeemed nature—better to say, for our present purposes, in the state of wounded nature—whereas we have no experiential knowledge of what the state of pure nature might have been; we can only depict it to ourselves in an abstract and imaginary manner, on the basis of our concept of human nature. As a result, a special difficulty arises in the discussion of the problem under consideration because we are liable to have our experience of the real man influence too much our very idea of the state of pure nature, so that we shall run a risk of minimizing the difference between the state of wounded nature and what the state of pure nature would have been.

Yet, on further consideration, I would rather believe that the difficulty—and the risk—in question occur in a reverse way. It is rather, it seems to me, in terms of our abstract notion of human nature that we have a tendency spontaneously to conceptualize our very experience of the real man, of man in the state of wounded nature, thus making our idea of this state resemble too much what man in the state of pure nature might have been. This is, I think, a deeper view of the matter. I understand in this way the paradoxical fact that, more often than not, when we are confronted in concrete experience with what man really is, we are suddenly astonished to find him, in actual fact, either much worse or much better —and, in certain cases, much worse and much better at the same time—than our image of him was. Thus it is that those who have the more articulate and elaborated abstract knowledge of man, namely, the moral philosopher and the moral theologian, are often like infants when it comes to dealing with man in real life and with his resources in goodness and in perversity. Neither philosophers nor theologians, but great sinners and great saints truly know man in the actual state of his nature.

A second question has to do with the notion of moral philosophy adequately taken. To my mind, it seems clear that moral philosophy must take into account these theological data relating to the various states of human nature. For, in fact, as a result of the present state of human nature, man has more propensity to evil than the man of pure nature by reason of the original sin and of the concupiscence which remains even in the just; and, on the other hand, he has incomparably stronger weapons for good, by reason of divine grace, with the organism of internal energies and the change in moral climate involved. Therefore, if the moral philosopher is to deal with the existential, the *real* man, he has to take this situation into account. He must not deal only with a man of pure nature—the man of pure nature is a mere possibility, an abstract possibility; he is not the man who actually *is*.

### *The theological notion of the various "states" in the historical development of mankind*

3. Here again, as in the next section also, we are learning from theology; yet, this time, we are coming closer to the subject matter of the philosophy of history. For

we have to do no longer with the various states of human nature with respect to sin and to divine grace, but with the various *historical* states of the existential man, as theology sees them: the "state of nature," for instance, the state of Abraham—that is, the moral regime or state of human kind before the written law; the "state of the Ancient Law"; and the "state of the New Law." The second state concerned especially the Jewish people, the two others have a universal bearing. The distinction between these three historical states, which is rooted in St. Paul's teachings, and in which mediaeval theologians were deeply interested, refers to the theology of history. We may say that St. Paul was the founder of the theology of history, especially with his basic doctrine (Rom., 3, 4) on the transition from the state of the Law (the Ancient Law) to the state of Gospel freedom (the New Law.)

To sum up St. Paul's teaching:[2] the Law is holy because it is the revealed expression of the wisdom of God. But while the Law makes us know evil, it does not give us the strength to avoid evil. And by making evil known, the Law is, for evil, an occasion for tempting us; and the wages of evil is death. In short, the Law is holy but it bears death with it. And Christ has freed us of the *regimen* of the Law because His grace, which makes us participate in the very life and sanctity of God, has now

[2] See my book *The Living Thoughts of St. Paul* (New York: Longmans, Green, 1941).

become revealed and manifested. We are no longer held to the multitude of ceremonial precepts nor to the juridical rules of the Mosaic Law; we are held to other ceremonial precepts less onerous and less numerous. And while we are ever held to the moral precepts of the Law, we are held thereto as to the requirements of the very life and freedom which are within us, not as to requirements which (as long as only the Law, and not Christ's grace, is relied upon) do us violence and exceed our capacity. Thus the New Law is less burdensome than the Old Law, though it prescribes a more difficult purity and holiness. If the New Law requires many less things beyond the prescriptions of the natural law, and many less ceremonial observances than the Old Law, in return it requires that which is the most difficult of all: purity in the hidden movements and internal acts of the soul. (And it demands that we nurture the *spirit* of the counsels of the Gospel.) But love makes light the yoke of this higher perfection.

Thus it must be said that we are no longer "under the Law," which is to say that we are quit of the regimen of the Law. We are quit of that condition of humanity wherein the government of its actions had, as its basic rule, no longer the natural light and the internal promptings of conscience, as in the days of the Patriarchs, and not as yet the promulgation of the Gospel, as after Christ's coming, but the promulgation of the written law transmitted by Moses. We have passed under the regimen of the New Law, which is a law of freedom.

This is the teaching of St. Paul. And it is the first great teaching—a divinely inspired teaching—about the direction and meaning of the historical development of mankind.

## The destiny of the Jewish people

4. The problem with which we are confronted here deals with a particular segment of human history: the history and destiny of this particular people which is the Jewish people, and the part played by them in the history of mankind. In fact, there are really two problems to be considered. The first is theological in nature; it is the problem—or, rather, the mystery—of the *destiny of the Jewish people with respect to the Kingdom of God and the order of eternal salvation*. The Jews did not understand the transition from the regimen of the Ancient Law to the regimen of the New Law, which is a law of freedom; they stuck to the regimen of the Mosaic Law. And, according to St. Paul, we have here two main points: first, their misstep or lapse was permitted for the salvation of all mankind; and, second, they will be finally reintegrated. Let us read a few passages from chapters nine, ten and eleven of St. Paul's Epistle to the Romans:

> "What then shall we say? That the Gentiles who were not seeking after justice have attained to justice, but the justice that is of faith. But Israel, by seeking after the law of justice, is not come unto the law of

justice. Why so? Because they sought it not by faith, but as it were of works. For they stumbled at the stumbling-stone. As it is written: *Behold I lay in Zion a stumbling-stone and a rock of scandal. And whosoever believeth in him shall not be confounded.*"[3]

"But I say: Hath not Israel known? First, Moses saith: *I will provoke you to jealousy against that which is not a nation: against a foolish nation I will anger you.* But Isaias is bold, and saith: *I was found by them that did not seek me. I appeared only to them that asked not after me.* But to Israel he saith: *All the day long have I spread my hands to a people that believeth not and contradicteth me.*"[4]

"I say then: Did God cast off his people? God forbid. . . .[5]

"I say then: Have they so stumbled, that they should fall? God forbid! But by their lapse salvation is come to the Gentiles, that they may be emulous of them. Now if the misstep of them is the riches of the world and the diminution of them the riches of the Gentiles: how much more the fulness of them? For I say to you, Gentiles: As indeed the Apostle of the Gentiles, I will honour my ministry. If, by any means, I may provoke to emulation them who are my flesh and may save some of them. For if the dispossession of them hath been the reconciliation of the world, what shall the reintegration

---

[3] Rom. 9, 30-33. This is taken from the Douay version of St. Paul's epistle, with a few words modified to make the sense clearer.
[4] Rom. 10, 19-21.
[5] Rom. 11, 1.

of them be, but life from the dead? For if the first fruit
be holy, so is the lump also: and if the root be holy, so
are the branches. And if some of the branches be broken
and thou, being a wild olive, wert ingrafted among
them and with them partakest of the root and of the
fatness of the olive tree: boast not against the branches.
And if thou boast, still it is not thou that bearest the
root, but the root thee. Thou wilt say then: branches
were broken off that I might be grafted in. Well: because of unbelief they were broken off. Thou standest
by faith. Be not highminded, but fear. For if God hath
not spared the natural branches, fear lest perhaps also he
spare not thee. See then the goodness and the severity
of God: towards them indeed that are fallen, the
severity; but towards thee, the goodness of God, if thou
abide in goodness. Otherwise thou also shalt be cut off.
And they also, if they abide not still in unbelief, shall
be grafted in; for God is able to graft them in again.
For if thou wert cut out of the wild olive tree, which is
natural to thee; and, contrary to nature, wert grafted
into the good olive tree: how much more shall they
that are the natural branches be grafted into their own
olive tree?

"For I would not have you ignorant, brethren, of
this mystery (lest you should be wise in your own
conceits) that blindness in part has happened in Israel,
until the fulness of the Gentiles should come in. And
so all Israel shall be saved, as it is written: *There shall
come out of Zion, he that shall deliver and shall turn
away ungodliness from Jacob. And this is to them my
covenant:* when I shall take away their sins. As touching the Gospel, indeed they are enemies for your sake;

but as touching the election, they are beloved for the sake of the fathers. For the gifts and the calling of God are without repentance. For as you also in times past did not believe God, but now have obtained mercy, through their unbelief: So these also have not believed, for your mercy, that they also may obtain mercy. For God hath concluded all in unbelief, that he may have mercy on all."[6]

Thus St. Paul states, apropos this particular mystery of Israel, a basic law (it is a revealed datum; it has nothing to do with philosophy as such) in human history— a basic law which he considered the most profound secret of divine Providence, and the meaning of which we can grasp only in the light of the infinite transcendence of Subsisting Love. You remember his saying: "Oh, the depth of the riches of the wisdom and of the knowledge of God! How incomprehensible are his judgments, and how unsearchable his ways!" (Rom. 11, 33). And he insists on this in three texts: "the Scripture shut up all things under sin, that by the faith of Jesus Christ, the promise might be given to those who believe." (Gal. 3, 22); "where the offense has abounded, grace has abounded yet more." (Rom. 5, 20); and, at the end of the long passage cited above, "God hath concluded all in unbelief, that he may have mercy on all." (Rom. 11, 32).

This law, which made St. Paul kneel down in adora-

6 Rom. 11, 11-32.

tion before the inscrutable wisdom of God, appeared to him, in a flash of light, especially with respect to the mystery of Israel. But it has a universal import. It is the most important datum of revealed wisdom with respect to human history, the unique key to the whole business of our long agonies, an insight into the relationship between the advance of mankind in time and the eternal purposes of the transcendent God, which the philosopher of history, too, should look at with clear-sighted awe, and hold as absolutely fundamental.

Hegel completely misunderstood this law, but he was aware of it in his own perverse way. He understood it in the very sense against which St. Paul took care to put us on our guard—that is, in the sense that evil would be *necessary* from a superior point of view, a divine point of view, in order to have good; sin would be necessary, from the point of view of the wisdom of history, in order to have this superabundance of goodness of which St. Paul speaks. And thus God—Hegel's immanent God, making himself through human history—would be the prime initiator of evil, entirely steeped in the mud and blood of the self-movement of mankind, because in the last analysis He would need evil in order to be; and the existence of evil—of evil to be overcome and reconciled —would be as necessary as God is.

But St. Paul does not speak of any necessity, and the very idea of a necessity for evil involved in God's pur- poses—and then let's do evil in order to cooperate with

God and his highest purposes[7]—is in his eyes sheer blasphemy. *Absit!* What he means to say is that God turns to a better purpose evil which He permits but in no way wills or causes, and whose first initiator is only the freedom of the creature. And this is the very triumph of God's wisdom and love, and the supreme meaning of human history, to have grace and mercy superabound there where, through the free *nihilation* of the human will, frustrating God's "antecedent" will, the offense abounded.

The prophetical element—that of the final reintegration of the Jewish people—contained in St. Paul's aforementioned texts played a great part in the theological speculation of the Middle Ages and in every discussion of Christian eschatology. In his commentary on the Gospel of St. John,[8] St. Thomas explains, in connection with the running of the Apostles Peter and John to the tomb of the Lord, that the two peoples, the Jewish people and the Gentile people, are symbolized at the tomb by the two Apostles. They simultaneously run to Christ through the ages, the Gentiles by their natural law, the Jews by their written law. The Gentiles, like Peter, who arrives second at the sepulchre, arrive later

---

[7] "What shall we say, then? Shall we continue in sin, that grace may abound? God forbid! For we that are dead to sin, how shall we live any longer therein?" Rom., 6: 1-2.

[8] Cf. St. Thomas Aquinas (in Reginald's transcr.), *In Joan.*, cap. 20, lect 1. The source is St. Gregory, *Homil. XXII in Evangelia*, n. 2, P. L., LXXVI, 1175.

at the knowledge of Jesus Christ. But, like Peter, they are the first to enter. The Jewish people, the first to know the mystery of the Redemption, will only be the last to be converted to the faith of Christ. 'Then,' says the Gospel, 'John went in.' Israel shall not remain eternally at the threshold of the sepulchre. After Peter shall have gone in, John himself will go in, for at the end the Jews also will be gathered into the faith.

The coming of this future event was considered unquestionable by the mediaeval theology of history. Let us add that in the second commentary on the *Song of Songs*, attributed to Thomas Aquinas, the author admits a division of the history of Christian times into three ages: first, Christian antiquity, which lasted about eight centuries; then, the Christian modern age (he speaks of the thirteenth century Church as "the modern church"); and, finally, the third age, not yet begun, whose most characteristic sign will be the reintegration of Israel.

5. The second problem having to do with Israel is the problem of *the destiny of the Jewish people with respect to the temporal history of the world and before their own final reintegration*. And here we have an aspect of the mystery of Israel that is more philosophical than theological. What is the meaning of the Diaspora? What is the meaning of the persecutions the Jews have suffered in the Christian world? What is the meaning of their own mission in the world? I think it is possible for

philosophical reflection, under the guidance of St. Paul's doctrine, to get at some conclusions.

I have already tackled this problem in an essay, "The Mystery of Israel," in my book *Ransoming the Time*. My point is that Israel is, analogically, a kind of Mystical Body; it is not only a people, but a people endowed with a mission which pertained to the very order of the redemption of mankind. And Israel's mission continues in a certain manner—no longer as an "ecclesial" mission—after its lapse, because it cannot help being the chosen people, for the gifts of God are without repentance, and the Jews are still beloved because of their fathers. So we might say that whereas the Church is assigned the task of the supernatural and supra-temporal saving of the world, to Israel is assigned, in the order of temporal history and its own finalities, the work of the *earthly leavening* of the world. Israel is here—to tell the truth, it is not *of* the world, but it is at the deepest core of the world—to irritate the world, to prod it, to move it. It teaches the world to be dissatisfied and restless so long as it has not God, so long as it has not justice on earth. Its indestructible hope stimulates the live forces of history.

Of course, this aspect does not make us disregard the sociological, economic, and other empirical aspects that we have to take into account when we try to understand the earthly destinies of Israel, or the moral cancer which is anti-Semitism, or the meaning of Zionism. But the philosophical aspect I just stressed—for it is philosophical, though enlightened by St. Paul's teaching (it's an example of what I have called moral philosophy adequately taken)—remains primary, and it casts light upon the other aspects. It cannot be disregarded.

New problems (I merely mention them) of great importance for the philosopher of history relate now to the founding of the State of Israel; its relation to the Diaspora—the relation between the Jews who are citizens of the State of Israel and the Jews who are citizens of other nations; its relation to the Moslem and the Christian areas of civilization; and the chances for and against its possible development as a state at the same time secular, democratic, with equal rights for all, but also religiously inspired and entrusted with a spiritual mission.

### The false Hegelian and Comtian laws of various states or stages

6. Both Hegel and Auguste Comte made use of this notion of states or stages which I employed above. Though their views relate, in my opinion, to a false philosophy of history, I would at least mention them here, for we can be instructed by wrong views, too.

According to Hegel, there are the three stages of the objective mind or spirit—the stage of abstract right; the stage of morality of conscience or subjective morality

(*Moralität*); and the stage of social morality (*Sittlich-keit*) or of the advent of the State. Now, of course, for Hegel these three stages are more metaphysical than historical. They don't refer essentially to historical succession. Yet such dialectical progress is revealed or manifested in the consciousness of mankind in a particularly significant manner at certain moments of the historical evolution. For instance, abstract right was typically manifested at the time of the Roman Empire; the morality of conscience or subjective morality in the centuries of Catholicism, and still more in the eighteenth century Enlightenment; whereas the third and final stage, the stage where all antinomies are resolved, appears in history when the German Protestant community takes political form, and the State emerges as the objectivation of the Divine—of that Divine which the young Hegel contemplated in Napoleon, the old Hegel in the Prussian State.

Another erroneous notion of the various states in human history—a notion which was quite famous during the nineteenth century—is Auguste Comte's notion of what he called "la loi des trois états," the law of the three stages or states. For Comte, mankind and the human mind passed successively through the *theological*, the *metaphysical*, and the *positive* state. In the theological state, everything was explained by supernatural beings and wills; in the metaphysical state, abstract occult causes took the place of supernatural beings, and everything was referred to vital forces, substantial forms, etc.; and finally, in the positive state, science is the unique rule—everything is to be understood in the light of sense-verified science, and both "wills" and "causes" must be replaced by "laws" or invariable relations between phenomena.

I would merely remark that this is indeed a quite interesting false generalization: on the one hand it was possible to find inductively (as regards the ways in which the human mind endeavored to interpret the phenomena of nature and to decipher sense-experience) some indications for such a construction; but, on the other hand, any inductive result was understood and conceptualized in the light of an erroneous philosophy, namely, positivist philosophy, for which *"everything is relative,* here is the only absolute principle," and there is *no other knowledge* than the knowledge of phenomena and the deciphering of sense-experience. From a genuinely historical point of view the *loi des trois états* is, even in the field of the knowledge of phenomena, a questionable and oversimplified generalization. But it is pure sophistry to claim that theology and metaphysics are done away with because a thunderbolt is not to be explained as an effect of some supernatural anger or of some "occult qualities."

*The law of the passage from the "magical"*
*to the "rational" regime or state*
*in the history of human culture*

7. This distinction, which I simply indicated at the beginning of this chapter, refers—at least, I think so— to a genuine philosophy of history. It is a philosophical distinction founded on, and interpreting, inductive data afforded by anthropology.[9] In an essay on *Sign and Symbol*,[10] written many years ago, I submitted that a distinction should be made between the *logical* sign, which speaks primarily to the intellect, and the *magical* sign, which speaks primarily to the imagination. My working hypothesis was the notion of functional condition or existential state, in the sense in which I have used the term "state" in this book. I was pointing to a fundamental distinction between the state of our developed cultures and another state or existential condition in which, for psychic and cultural life as a whole, the last word rests with the imagination, as the supreme and final law. In this latter state, the intellect is doubtless present, and with all its inherent principles and laws, but in a way it is not *free*—it is tied up, bound to the imagination. That is

[9] I would stress that no philosophy of history can be complete without anthropology—anthropology is a basic consideration for the philosopher of history.

[10] See *Quatre essais sur l'esprit dans sa condition charnelle* (1939; Paris: Alsatia, 1956, new ed.), Chapter II; *Ransoming the Time* (New York: Charles Scribner's Sons, 1941), Chapter IX.

the state I am calling the *magical* regime or state of psychic and cultural life.

I would note that this working hypothesis succeeded in reconciling opposed points of view in a particularly controversial field. A few years before his death, Professor Lévy-Bruhl was so kind as to write and express his agreement with me on this point: "as you put it quite rightly, primitive mentality is a *state* of human mentality, and I can accept the characteristics through which you define it."

Allow me to quote now the testimony of the great Polish anthropologist, Bronislaw Malinowski: "I have chosen to face the question of primitive man's rational knowledge directly: watching him at his principal occupations, seeing him pass from work to magic and back again, entering into his mind, listening to his opinions. The whole problem might have been approached through the avenue of language, but this would have led us too far into questions of logic, semasiology, and theory of primitive languages. Words which serve to express general ideas such as *existence, substance,* and *attribute, cause* and *effect,* the *fundamental* and the *secondary;* words and expressions used in complicated pursuits like sailing, construction, measuring and checking; numerals and quantitative descriptions, correct and detailed classifications of natural phenomena, plants and animals—all this would lead us exactly to the same conclusion: that primitive man can observe and think, and that he possesses, embodied in his language, systems of methodical though rudimentary knowledge."

And Malinowski continues: "Similar conclusions could be drawn from an examination of those mental schemes and physical contrivances which could be described as diagrams or formulas. Methods of indicating the main points of the compass, arrangements of stars into constellations, co-ordination of these with the seasons, naming of moons in the year, of quarters in the moon—all these accomplishments are known to the simplest savages. Also they are all able to draw diagrammatic maps in the sand or dust, indicate arrangements by placing small stones, shells, or sticks on the ground, plan expeditions or raids on such rudimentary charts. By co-ordinating space and time they are able to arrange big tribal gatherings and to combine vast tribal movements over extensive areas. . . . The use of leaves, notched sticks, and similar aids to memory is well known and seems to be almost universal. All such 'diagrams' are means of reducing a complex and unwieldy bit of reality to a simple and handy form. They give man a relatively easy mental control over it. As such are they not—in a very rudimentary form no doubt—fundamentally akin to developed scientific formulas and 'models,' which are also simple and handy paraphrases of a complex or abstract reality, giving the civilized physicist mental control over it?"[11]

---

[11] Bronislaw Malinowski: *Magic, Science and Religion* (Anchor Books), pp. 33-34. See also Pierre Lecomte du Noüy's *Human Destiny* (Signet Books), Book III, especially pp. 79-80.

The intellect in primitive man is of the same kind as ours. It may even be move alive in him than in some civilized men. But the question with which we are concerned is that of its existential conditions, the existential regime or state under which it operates. In primitive man the intellect is in a general way involved with, and dependent on, the imagination and its savage world. This kind of mental regime is one in which acquaintance with nature is experienced and lived through with an intensity and to an extent we cannot easily picture. I observed in the previous chapter that in passing from the myths of the primitive man to our rational or logical regime there were surely losses, compensating for the greater gains achieved by such a progress.

The magical state is a state of inferiority, but it is by no means despicable. It is the state of mankind in its infancy, a fertile state through which we have had to pass. And I think that anthropologists should recognize that under this regime humanity enriched itself with many vital truths, which were known by way of dream or divinatory instinct, and by actual participation in the thing known—not in a conceptual, rational manner. It is extremely difficult for us to imagine now what can have been the functioning of the human mind in such a state. It is a difficulty analogous to that which we experience when we try to penetrate the mental life of animals. Whatever *we* picture to ourselves is in fact bathed in intelligence, and in intelligence which is free, which has the upper hand over imagination. Therefore we have

great trouble in depicting to ourselves any state in which
—in the case of primitive man—imagination had the
upper hand over the intellect; or in which—in the case
of the animal—there is knowledge, but merely sensitive
knowledge: knowledge by way of the senses, which
admittedly are capable, in superior vertebrates, of *re-
sembling* intelligence to a great extent. It is really impossible for a man to imagine how a dog is "thinking."
But nevertheless there is a dog-knowledge which exists
as a matter of fact, and is the object of the psychology
of animals. We experience a similar difficulty when it
comes to the magical state proper to the mental activity
of the primitive man, a state utterly different from our
logical state, and in which the imagination was the queen
of the human mind. We might call our present state
a daylight or solar state because it is bound up with
the luminous and regular life of the intellect. And the
magical state might be called a nocturnal state, because
it is bound up with the fluid and twilight life of the
imagination.

8. Here I would like to propose some remarks on
positivism and Comte's law of the three states. From the
positivist point of view one is led to say that the mathematical and physico-mathematical sciences, and all the
multifarious sciences of phenomena, constitute the only
function of truth and real knowledge in human thought,
and that, therefore, religion, mystical experience, meta-

physics, and poetry are, in the civilized mind, an inheritance from the primitive and "pre-logical" mentality. This is a major tenet in the positivists' philosophy of history. These types of mental activity are but metamorphoses of ancient magic—perhaps justifiable in the practical and emotional order, but directly opposed, as is magic itself, to the line of science and truth.[12] The era of science has succeeded to the era of magic, and magic and science are essentially inimical and incompatible. For Bergson, I may add, magic and science are similarly inimical and incompatible. "Magic is the reverse of science," he wrote in *The Two Sources* because, for Bergson, also, science consists entirely in the mathematical explanation of matter. Yet in Bergson's view, science, at least science in the process of being born, always co-existed with magic. And science does not exhaust the function of truth and real knowledge in human thought. Other functions—religion, mystical experience, metaphysics, and poetry—are also functions of truth, and more profound ones. But for Bergson, as for the positivists, these things are at right angles to the line of science, and they spring from the same vital centre as magic. Magic and religion have a common origin, from which they developed in opposite directions—magic

[12] I remember that Lévy-Bruhl sent a copy of his first book on primitive mentality to a friend of his, the Belgian poet Verhaeren. Verhaeren wrote to Lévy-Bruhl that he was delighted to read the book because he found in it a complete description of his own mentality. Well, this was more of a criticism than a compliment.

in the direction of illusion, myth-making, and laziness; and religion (what Bergson called "dynamic religion") in the direction of heroism and of truth.

Now the distinction which I have proposed between the magical and the rational states of the human mind and culture differs at once from the positivist and from the Bergsonian positions. To my mind, our modern science of phenomena is only one of the possible forms of science, only one of the degrees of knowledge. Moreover, science, philosophy, metaphysics, like religion and mysticism, and like poetry, are destined to grow up together. In the nocturnal state, the magical state of the primacy of the dream and of the imagination, they were inchoate, more or less fused or confused, but they were there. Once the threshold of the daylight state of the primacy of the intellect and the Logos was passed, they became more and more differentiated from each other. It is not true that "the era of science has succeeded the era of magic"—what is true is that the state of Logos has succeeded the state of Magic—for all the mental and cultural functions of the human being existed in the state of magic, and they now exist in the state of logical thought. Science, like religion, existed in the nocturnal state before it existed in the daylight state. So, one cannot say that there is nothing in common between magic and science, and that magic is the reverse of science. One can only say that the magical state of science—of that rudimentary science of the tribal man which was alluded to in Malinowski's remarks quoted above—is in opposition to the logical state of civilized man's science. Thus my point is that all human thought, with its great and at first undifferentiated primordial ramifications, passes through a diversity of existential conditions or states. The science of the primitive man was science, and it was such in the state of magic—primitive man had a certain knowledge of nature, real and workable, though different from ours. This knowledge made use of certain connections of physical causality, and it formulated them in an intelligibly manageable manner, all the while immersing them in a kind of sacral empiricism, and in a general way of thinking dominated by the magical sign. Science left this condition when it passed over the threshold of the Logos-dominated regime of thought and of culture. Now, in our civilized times, the residues of magical knowing are taken over, by virtue of a process of abnormal integration, by a pseudo-science—the occultism, or the occult "sciences," of civilized man—utterly different from the magic of primitive man, and which will carry with it certain pathological characteristics for intellectual life (as happens for affective life in certain cases of infantile retrogression among adults).

Similar observations may be made with respect to religion. Religion was at first in a magical or nocturnal state, and then it passed under a new regime, the daylight state of human thought and culture. The religion

of civilized humanity crossed the threshold of this daylight state either by a transformation into more or less
rationalized mythology (as in Greece), or by a process
of metaphysical elaboration (as in India), or by forms
of revelation adapted to such a state (as in Judaeo-
Christian monotheism). And, just as in certain forms of
pseudo-knowledge, so in certain pseudo-religious phenomena to which the civilized man is liable to fall prey,
residues of the magical state will appear, taken over, by
virtue of a process of abnormal integration, by supersti-
tious notions and imagery, wherein the part played by
pathology is far greater than in magical religion itself.

### The law of the progress of moral conscience

9. I consider this to be a most important law in the
philosophy of history. In its essence and even in its
value, the rectitude and purity of moral conscience are
independent of the explicit knowledge of all particular
moral laws. We realize this if we think, for example, of
the three states distinguished by theology in the history
of mankind.[13] Abraham was a great saint, a saint of
incomparable stature. But he did not know that certain
actions which we condemn today were prohibited by
natural law. Hence we must conclude that mankind's
state of nature was not a state in which natural moral

[13] See above, pp. 82-85.

laws were perfectly known and practised.[14] As a matter of fact, the precise knowledge of these natural moral laws—with the exception of the self-evident primary principle, *good is to be done and evil to be avoided*—is acquired slowly and with more or less difficulty. I would say that the equipment necessary to know the particular precepts of natural law exists within us—it is made up of the essential tendencies and inclinations of our nature. But a very long experience is required to have the corresponding knowledge through connaturality take actual form.

In other words, our knowledge of moral laws is progressive in nature. The sense of duty and obligation was always present, but the explicit knowledge of the various norms of natural law grows with time. And certain of these norms, like the law of monogamy, were known rather late in the history of mankind, so far as it is accessible to our investigation. Also, we may think that the knowledge of the particular precepts of natural law in all of their precise aspects and requirements will continue to grow until the end of human history.

I think that this progress of moral conscience as to the explicit knowledge of natural law is one of the least questionable examples of progress in mankind. Allow me to stress that I am not pointing to any progress in human

[14] See Raïssa Maritain, *Histoire d'Abraham ou les premiers âges de la conscience morale* (Paris: Desclée De Brouwer, 1947); Engl. trans.: *Abraham and the Ascent of Conscience*, in *The Bridge*, vol. I (New York: Pantheon Books, 1955).

moral behavior (or to any progress in the purity and sanctity of conscience, for Abraham, again, was a very great saint, with an absolutely pure heart). I am pointing to a progress of moral conscience as to the *knowledge* of the particular precepts of natural law.[15] This progress in knowledge can take place at the same time as a worsening in the conduct of a number of men, but that is another question. Take, for instance, the notion of slavery. We are now aware that slavery is contrary to the dignity of the human person. And yet there are totalitarian States which enslave the human being. But, nevertheless, they would not like to acknowledge this fact—that's why propaganda is so necessary—because there is a common awareness in mankind today that slavery is contrary to the dignity of man.

We may cite a few of the other examples of this progress in moral conscience. One is the notion of the treatment to be given to prisoners of war. For many, many centuries, and even Christian centuries, it was considered quite normal to kill prisoners of war. No difference was recognized between an enemy soldier in combat and one who had been taken prisoner. If a prisoner of war was granted life, this was considered a favor which was legitimately paid for by slavery. But now we have

---

[15] I would recall here St. Jerome's comment in reference to the patriarchs and the limited knowledge of natural law which prevailed in their time (with particular reference to polygamy): "Abraham was much holier than I am," he said, "but my *state* is better." (I quote St. Jerome from memory; there is a similar remark in St. Augustine, *De bono conjugali*, XXIII, n. 28.)

a completely different view of our obligations towards prisoners of war. Another example is the notion of child labor. At the beginning of the industrial age, child labor was considered quite legitimate. But now we have other ideas about this matter, and they are surely more conformable to natural law. Still another example is the notion of human labor itself. The notion that human labor is impossible without the whip of destitution— a notion quite widespread in the nineteeth century— seemed at that moment to be in accordance with natural law. Even religion and a misreading of Adam's punishment in *Genesis*, were made to contribute to this notion. But now we realize the great error in such a conception. And again: the notion that authority cannot be exercized without a lot of ruthlessness, and without the suppression of any human fellowship between the one who commands and the one who obeys, is another notion which seemed obvious at one time, and which is now considered wrong by a progress in our awareness of what human nature basically requires in our mutual relations and in the moral atmosphere of our living together. Finally, may I say that we probably are still in the dark about the part normally to be played in temporal and political matters themselves by laws which deal directly with spiritual life, such as the law of mutual forgiveness.

*10.* So much for the progress in our awareness of the more and more particular requirements of natural law.

If it is a question, on the other hand, of a certain primal, extremely general and undifferentiated knowledge of the basic precepts of natural law, we have to elaborate in connection with anthropology the notion of what I would call the *fundamental dynamic schemes* of natural law, the meaning of which is highly undetermined. They are but general tendential forms or frameworks, such as can be obtained by the first, the "primitive" achievements of knowledge through inclination. We may think, for instance, of such general and undifferentiated principles as: to take a man's life is not like taking another animal's life; the family group has to comply with some fixed pattern; sexual intercourse has to be contained within given limitations; we are bound to look at the Invisible; we are bound to live together under certain rules and prohibitions. I think that these five general regulations correspond to the basic inclinations of which St. Thomas speaks in his treatise on natural law.[16] And they are subject, I would submit, to a much more universal aware-

---

[16] "In man there is, first of all, an inclination to good in accordance with the nature which he possesses in common with all substances: inasmuch as every substance tends to preserve its own being, according to its nature. . . . Secondly, there is in man an inclination to things which appertain to him more specially according to the nature that he shares with the animals: and in virtue of this inclination, those things are said to belong to the natural law 'which nature has taught all animals,' such as sexual intercourse, education of offspring, and so forth. Thirdly, there is in man an inclination to good, according to the nature of his reason, which nature is proper to him. Thus, man has a natural inclination to know the truth about God, and to live in society." *Summa theol.* I-II, 94, 2.

ness—everywhere and in every time—than would appear to a superficial glance. It is true that there is an immense amount of relativity and variability to be found in the particular rules, customs, and standards in which, among all peoples of the earth, human reason has expressed its knowledge of these most basic aspects of natural law. But if we consider the dynamic schemes in their entire generality we see that they were always recognized in one way or another.

And now, as a corollary to my reflections on the progress of moral conscience, I would emphasize that moral philosophy presupposes moral experience, the historical experience of mankind. Moral philosophy, as indeed all philosophical knowledge, comes about through concepts and judgments. It supposes a developed rational knowledge. It entails a scientific justification of moral values by a demonstrative determination of what is consonant with reason, and of the proper ends of the human essence and of human society. But it is a kind of afterknowledge. The moral philosopher submits to critical examination, elucidates, sorts out, justifies, re-interprets, formulates in a more systematic or more pungent manner the natural morality of mankind, I mean the moral standards and regulations which are spontaneously known to human reason in such or such an age of culture. As a result, it is rather infrequent that a moral philosopher is in advance with respect to his time.

In other words, moral philosophy is a reflective knowledge, and in this we have a token of its difference from metaphysical knowledge. Metaphysics is not a reflective knowledge—it is not a reflection on common sense. It states its own truths, and nobody can judge a metaphysician, except in the name of a higher wisdom. But any kind of virtuous man, even one completely ignorant in philosophy, can judge a moral philosopher, if the moral philosopher teaches something wrong. I see in this a sign that moral philosophy is a reflective knowledge. And therefore, while it can happen, of course, that a moral philosopher may have broader horizons than the common people of his time, and may see things that they do not see, nevertheless, in general, the work of theoretical reflection cannot replace in moral matters the slow advance of consciousness, conscience, and experience in mankind. And this means not only an advance in rational knowledge, but primarily an advance in our lived awareness of our basic inclinations—an advance which may be conditioned by social changes. Thus for many centuries moral philosophers and common consciousness stressed the obligations of man prescribed by natural law. But there are also rights of man, which were, of course, implicitly recognized, especially by Christian thinkers. Yet it seems to me that it was necessary to wait until the eighteenth century, and the related social changes in human history, to have the basic inclinations on which an explicit awareness of these rights depends liberated in us—a fact which had an impact both on the common consciousness of mankind and on the rational consideration of moral and social philosophers.

### The law of the passage from "sacral" to "secular" or "lay" civilizations

*11.* The distinction between "sacral" and "secular" civilizations has a universal bearing. Yet—by reason of the very distinction between the things that are Caesar's and the things that are God's—it is with Christianity that this distinction has taken its full historical importance. It is, therefore, but natural that in the present discussion I should refer to sacral Christian civilization and to secular Christian civilization. There was a sacral age, the age of mediaeval Christendom, mainly characterized, on the one hand, by the fact that the unity of faith was a prerequisite for political unity, and that the basic frame of reference was the unity of that social body, religio-political in nature, which was the *respublica Christiana;* and, on the other hand, by the fact that the dominant dynamic idea was the idea of fortitude at the service of justice. The modern age, on the contrary, is not a sacral but a secular age. The order of temporal society has gained complete differentiation, and full autonomy in its own sphere, which is something normal in itself, required by the Gospel's distinction between God's and Caesar's domains. But that normal process was accompanied—and spoiled—by a most aggressive and stupid process of insulation from, and finally rejection of, God and the Gospel in the sphere of social and political life. The fruit of this we can contemplate today in the theocratic atheism of the Communist State.

Yet the fact remains that, as a result of the process of differentiation I just alluded to, the dominant dynamic idea of modern civilization is not the idea of fortitude at the service of justice, but rather the idea of the conquest of freedom and of social conditions conformable to human dignity. On the other hand, the root requirement for a sound mutual cooperation between the Church and the body politic is no longer the unity of a religio-political body, as the *respublica Christiana* of the Middle Ages was, but the very unity of the human person, simultaneously a member of the body politic and of the Church. And the unity of religion is not a prerequisite for political unity. Men subscribing to diverse religious or non-religious creeds have to share in and work for the same political or temporal common good.

This distinction between sacral and secular civilizations is a quite simple distinction. But once it has been formulated in rational terms, it provides us with a key to interpret the life and cultural standards of the Middle Ages in comparison with our own ways of life and cultural standards.[17] In other books (especially *True Hu-*

---

[17] I was most gratified to see this distinction used and emphasized by Msgr. Charles Journet in his great work, *L'Eglise du Verbe*

*manism* and *Man and the State*) I have laid stress on its importance with respect to a correct interpretation of the relation between Church and State in our times, and to a correct formulation of the concrete historical ideal appropriate to the coming age of civilization.

I would suggest that the same distinction could also serve as a key to the discussion of other areas of civilization. Thus, if we were dealing with a complete philosophy of history, we should consider in what sense Indian civilization is a sacral civilization. This is a great problem. Another great problem—one with practical as well as theoretical implications—is whether a sacral civilization like the Moslem one can become secular. Is it possible to have the same kind of development or evolution in the Moslem world as in the Christian world? Still another problem, which has already been touched upon, has to do with the State of Israel. As a State, a modern and democratic State, it cannot be sacral. But, on the other hand, to be a Jew means essentially to belong to a certain religious tradition, which is still at work hiddenly —even in those who have repudiated any definite creed —and which will probably take some kind of new

---

*Incarné* (Paris: Desclée De Brouwer, 1941). See Vol. I, pp. 269-425 (Eng. tr., *The Church of the Word Incarnate*, Vol. I, London and New York: Sheed and Ward, 1955, pp. 214-330). It is good to have a notion elaborated in the field of the philosophy of history thus sanctioned by a theologian. Again, there must be cooperation between the philosophy of history and the theology of history. They are distinct, but they must not be separated.

vitality in many of the Jews who are now re-grouped in the Promised Land. Now, how will the State of Israel solve this question? Can it be at the same time Jewish and secular? What kind of freedom will the Israelian citizens who have embraced the Christian faith enjoy in such a State? This is a big question, and one that relates both to the philosophy of history and to political practice.

Finally, I think that the distinction we just discussed may help us in our approach to antiquity. We know that in antiquity there was no distinction between the things that are Caesar's and the things that are God's. Religion was embodied in the gods of the city. So we cannot speak of Greek civilization, for instance, as a secular civilization. Nor was it sacral in the strict sense of this word. It was sacral, I would say, in a different though analogical sense, peculiar to polytheism, and moreover rather difficult to characterize. Some writers, for instance Henri Marrou,[18] are apt to speak of the early Greek conception of the city, even of the Platonic utopia, as "totalitarian." To my mind, this is an erroneous wording. I think that we should coin a special concept—Greek civilization was neither "totalitarian," nor "secular," nor "sacral" in the Christian or Moslem sense, but rather, I suggest, "hieropolitical."[19] It was hieropolitical because,

[18] See his excellent *Histoire de l'éducation dans l'antiquité* (Paris: Editions du Seuil, 1948), especially Parts I and II.
[19] See *supra*, p. 69.

on the one hand, the body politic was supreme in dignity (though bound to venerate the unwritten wisdom embodied in the cosmos), and, on the other hand, there was something sacred, something hieratic in the very notion of the political city, which was itself in charge of religious functions. This is but another example of the kind of questions which are within the province of the philosophy of history.

### The law of the political and social coming of age of the people

*12.* This law, which I shall point to in a brief manner (because in order to be fully elucidated it would require an entire book) deals with the progressive passage of the people, in the course of modern history, from a state of subjection to a state of self-government in political and social matters, in other words, to a regime of civilization characterized by the democratic cast of mind and democratic philosophy.

The change in question is, I think, still in its first phases, and in relation to it nations which are *de facto* contemporaneous find themselves at quite diverse historical stages. It was but natural that it should appear in political life before extending step by step to social life. Moreover, a normal development, called for by deep aspirations in human nature, was there preyed upon by a lot of wrong or perverse ideas which finally instigated the very opposite of democracy—the totalitarian State— and which imperil the democratic principle itself as long as it does not free itself completely of them.

The remark I wish to submit is that, considered in its normal and essential features, the political and social coming of age of the people was in itself a natural development—I mean, one which answered deep-seated demands of the order of nature, and in which certain requirements of natural law came to the fore; but in actual fact it is only under the action of the Gospel leaven, and by virtue of the Christian inspiration making its way in the depths of secular consciousness,[20] that the natural development in question took place. Thus it is that the democratic process, with its genuine, essential properties, and its adventitious ideological cockle, appeared first in that area of civilization which is the historical heir to mediaeval Western Christendom—and it was the more genuine, and is now the more live, where the temporal life of the community remains to a larger extent Christian-inspired.

But once the democratic process had appeared and prevailed in the area in question, it spontaneously spread, and keeps on spreading, over all other areas of civilization (except in those places where it is blocked by totali-

[20] See my book *Christianity and Democracy* (New York: Charles Scribner's Sons, 1944).

tarianism).[21] Such a spontaneous universal spreading of the democratic process is an obvious sign of its basically natural character, in the sense I pointed out a moment ago.

[21] And still the fact remains that willy-nilly, Communism, in the very use it makes of the phrase "people's democracy," cannot help paying tribute to the moral power of the democratic principle.

*Chapter 4*

# GOD AND THE MYSTERY
# OF THE WORLD

## God and history

*1.* There is no more fundamental problem for the philosophy of history than that of the relationship between divine freedom and human freedom in the shaping of history. As I have elsewhere discussed this problem at some length,[1] I shall give now only the briefest possible summary of my views on this question.

The first point to be emphasized is that God is absolutely *innocent*. He is in absolutely no way the cause of moral evil. Moral evil originates in man's free non-consideration of the rule, in man's free *nihilation*. Hence man is the first cause (negative cause, of course) of evil. Evil is the only thing (because it is not a *thing*) that can be done without God.[2] And the permission for such

---

[1] *Existence and the Existent* (New York: Pantheon Books, 1948), pp. 85-122.

[2] The bad *action* or *decision* is a sort of thing, or being, spoiled by that "privation" which is evil. In order to exist, it presupposes the general divine motion through which everything in the universe is activated. I am not speaking here of the bad action or decision *as action or decision*, but of the very *evil or privation* which spoils it.

nihilation is included in the fact that God gives a break-able motion or activation[3] toward good—that is to say, a motion or activation which can be broken if man freely slips away from it. Furthermore, there is a per-missive decree of God (involving the intention of some greater good) for the execution of the evil act.

Now, as regards the divine plan, we must hold that this plan is established, of course, from all eternity. But we must be aware that eternity is not a kind of divine time which precedes time. It is a limitless instant which indivisibly embraces the whole succession of time. All the moments of that succession are physically present in it. Thus "to foresee" is an improper phrase to use when speaking of God. We employ it because we project into His eternity the anteriority (in relation to future events) of the knowledge which *we would have* if *we* knew them *before* they happened. They are known to Him "al-ready," which is to say, always. He sees them as actually taking place at a given temporal instant which is present to His eternity. All things and all events in nature are known to Him at their first coming forth and in the eternal morning of His vision, because they are willed by Him, beyond all time, in the eternal instant with which their whole succession co-exists.

But when we deal with the world of freedom, and not

---

[3] I have proposed this expression "breakable motion or activation" as a kind of philosophical equivalent of the theological expression "sufficient grace."

only with the world of nature, when we deal with free existents, creatures endowed with freedom of choice, we must go still farther. We must say that in a certain fashion those creatures have their part in the very establishment of the eternal plan—not, indeed, by virtue of their power to act (here all they have they hold of God) but by virtue of their power to nihilate, to make the thing that is nothing, where they themselves, as I said above, are first causes. Free existents have their part in the establishment of God's plan, because in establishing that plan He takes account of their initiatives of nihilating.

In other words, God's eternal plan must not be conceived anthropomorphically as a kind of scenario written in advance. Suppose that the eternal plan were a scenario made in advance, i.e., *before*—not from above, in eternity, but in a time before time. Suppose that in this scenario it were written that Brutus should assassinate Caesar.[4] Then, when Brutus enters the stage of the world, either the Director will leave him truly free to have or not have the first initiative of sin, in which case Brutus might not murder Caesar and might thus frustrate the eternal plan—which is nonsense; or the Director will have arranged things in one way or another so that Brutus really does assassinate Caesar, and yet still commits the murder freely. But then how is one to get

[4] For the purpose of the argument, I assume that Brutus was a criminal.

around the fact that it would be God Who had the first initiative of the sin, and Who, if only by giving him a free hand, made the creature fall?

The true conception is that the divine plan is immutable *once fixed* from all eternity. But it is only fixed from all eternity *with account taken of the free default of man*, which God sees in His eternal present. Man enters thus into the eternal plan. Not in order to modify it! To say this would be an absurdity. He enters into its very composition and its eternal fixation by his power of saying: No. In the line of evil, it is the creature who is the first cause. Thus we may interpret in two ways the Gospel saying, "Without Me you can do nothing." It may be interpreted as relating to the line of good, and then it means: without God we can do nothing, i.e., without God we cannot do the slightest act in which there is being or goodness. Or it may be interpreted as relating to the line of evil, and then it means: without God we can do nothingness, i.e., without God we can make the thing which is nothing, we can introduce into action and being the nothingness which wounds them and which constitutes evil. The first initiative always comes from God in the case of good, and then the initiative of created liberty itself arises from the divine initiative. But because of the power of refusal, which naturally forms part of all created liberty, the first initiative always comes from the creature in the case of evil.

Thus we can form some idea of the drama of history,

or rather the drama of the superior, the sacred regions of history. Whatever is the part of the visible material which conditions it in the world of nature, history is made up above all of the crossing and intermingling, of the pursuit and conflict of uncreated liberty and created liberty. It is, as it were, invented at each moment of time by the accorded or disaccorded initiatives of these two freedoms—one in time, the other outside of time and knowing, from the heights of eternity, to which all moments of time are indivisibly present, the whole succession in a single glance. And the glory of the divine liberty is to create an even more beautiful work the more it allows the other liberty to unmake it, because from the abundance of destructions it alone can draw a superabundance of being. But we, who are lodged in the tapestry, see only the obscure entanglement of the threads which are knotted in our heart.

Such are, in brief summary, my views on the problem of the relationship between the defectible freedom of man and the eternal freedom of God—the problem that is, in my opinion, the absolutely primary problem for the philosopher of history.

### The world and its natural ends

2. What is the world? In a most general sense, it is the ensemble of created things, or of *all that which is not God*. Then, in a more restricted sense, it is our *material*

and visible universe. And then it is our *human* and moral universe, the cosmos of man, culture, and history, as they develop on earth, with all the mutual relations and tensions involved. The world, thus, constitutively belongs to the order of nature; and it is from the mere point of view of nature that we shall consider it first. Let me observe, in addition, that this *human* sense of the word *cosmos, mundus, the world,* is most appropriate: for in the material universe man, as an intelligent and free agent ("in the likeness of God") is *par excellence* the existent which is not God.

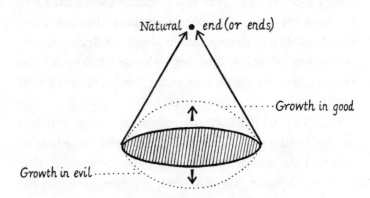

The world considered from the mere
point of view of nature

DIAGRAM NUMBER 2

Now I would propose a very simple diagram (Diagram Number 2). The circle indicates the world, and the shadow indicates that good and evil are intermingled in the world. The point indicates the natural end or ends of the world. The dotted line above represents the growth in good, and the one below the growth in evil—both of these growths being characteristic of the movement of history.

What can we say concerning the natural end of the world? In my opinion, we may say that this natural end is threefold. A first aspect of the natural end of world history is mastery over nature and the conquest of autonomy for mankind. We read in *Genesis*, 1:28: "And God blessed them, saying: Increase and multiply, and fill the earth, and subdue it, and rule over the fishes of the sea, and the fowls of the air, and all living creatures that move upon the earth." These words point to mastery over nature: *subdue the earth*. And we should never forget that there is such a natural end for the history of the world. It is something temporal and terrestrial, and it is a real end or aim of the world, and one even mentioned in the Bible. The philosopher may express the same thing in other words, if he reflects on the nature of man as a rational agent immersed in animality. He may say that this end is man's conquest of autonomy, his conquest of freedom in the sense of autonomy—liberation from bondage and coercion exercised by physical nature on this being who has an element of spirit in him, as well as liberation from enslavement by other men.

A second aspect is the development of the multifarious immanent or spiritual, self-perfecting activities of such a being, especially knowledge—all the various degrees of knowledge—and creative activity in art, and, as concerns moral activity, that progress in the knowledge of natural law which we mentioned in the previous chapter.

Finally, a third aspect of this natural end of the world may be brought out—I mean, the manifestation of all the potentialities of human nature. This, too, would follow from the fact that man is not a pure spirit but a spirit united to matter. It is normal for a spirit to manifest itself. And because man has so many hidden potentialities, it is normal that he reveal progressively this inner universe which is man himself. Here I would like to apply another word of the Gospel: "There is nothing hidden which shall not be made manifest."[5] And one may think, it seems to me, that the very shamelessness of contemporary literature, with its impure incentives and its ridiculous enslavement to fashion, has for all that a kind of eschatological meaning. It is a yielding to this urge to manifest what is in man. And, of course, it is when it veers to masochist forms that such an urge is the easier to release.

I have spoken of the threefold end of the world. The world advances toward it. But let us not forget that, as I have previously observed, there is a progress both in the direction of good and at the same time in the direction

[5] Matt., 10, 26; Luke, 8, 17.

of evil. All this concerns the natural order, the world considered in the mere perspective of nature.

### Christ's mystical body

3. But, as a matter of fact, we know that man has been called to another order and another life—to the supernatural order. And here we have another universe, the Church in the full and fully realistic theological sense of this word, which is synonymous with the Mystical Body of Christ, and, as Charles Journet puts it, with "the Kingdom of God in the state of pilgrimage and crucifixion"—a universe distinct from the world and in interrelation with it. The question of the various senses in which a man can belong to the Church has been thoroughly examined by Msgr. Journet in his work on the Church.[6] For our present purposes, and from our present point of view, it is enough to observe, in a quite simplified manner, that all men belong, in one sense or another, to the Church, or might be called, in one sense or another, the redeemed of the Church (redeemed in hope). There are, first of all, the visible members of the Church, those who belong to her by faith, by Baptism, and by adherence to the authority of the Vicar of Christ; if they are not, by reason of mortal sin, blocked members, love and suffering, in Christ's grace, make them actively participant, by virtue of their sacramental in-

[6] See *L'Eglise du Verbe Incarné*, Vol. II, pp. 1056-1114.

corporation in Christ, in His very work of redemption. There are, secondly, the invisible participants in the Church—those who do not have integral explicit faith but who are of good faith and good will, and who have initial faith,[7] inner grace and charity. And there are, finally, the potential participants in the Church—those who have neither faith, even initial, nor charity, nor the baptismal character, but who *can* receive grace and thereby share in the life of the Church.[8]

Therefore the universe of the Church, of the mystical body of Christ or the Kingdom of God, has at least potentially the same extension as the world. But it is a supernatural universe, living on grace and charity, and headed by Christ. Its end is the supernatural end, God and participation in the very life of God. And evil has no part in it; the Devil has no part in it. This is an essential point, which I shall try to elucidate later.[9] This universe of the Church is without stain, without rust: *sine macula, sine ruga.* I have indicated this in Diagram Number 3. The circle representing the Kingdom of God has no shadow, because this universe is spotless. The Kingdom of God is a holy universe; whereas the world,

---

[7] I mean that faith in God, "rewarder to them that seek him" (Hebr., 11, 6), in which all the other tenets of faith are implicitly contained.

[8] Cf. *Summa theol.*, III, 8, 4, ad 1: "Illi qui sunt infideles, etsi actu non sint de Ecclesia, sunt tamen de Ecclesia in potentia. Quae quidem potentia in duabus fundatur: primo quidem et principaliter in virtute Christi, quae est sufficiens ad salutem totius humani generis; secundario, in arbitrii libertate."

[9] See *infra*, pp. 141-142.

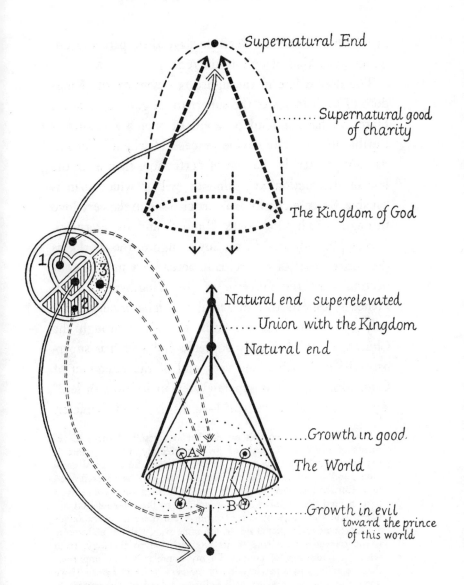

Supernatural End

Supernatural good
of charity

The Kingdom of God

1
2
3

Natural end  superelevated

Union with the Kingdom

Natural end

Growth in good

The World

A

B

Growth in evil
toward the prince
of this world

DIAGRAM NUMBER 3

in which evil and the devil do have their part and do-
minion, is a kind of unholy universe.

The dotted line in the figure representing the Kingdom of God indicates the supernatural good of charity.
Here we have a kind of good of which mankind is
capable by virtue of divine grace, and which is incomparably greater, in the line of perfection, than is, in the
line of destruction, any kind of evil of which man is
capable, because charity is a participation in the very love
through which God loves Himself, and us, eternally.

Now, as indicated in the lower figure, the world, as
the entire order of nature, is in actual fact in vital connection with the universe of the Kingdom of God.
Hence it appears that in actual fact it is ordained, not
only to its own natural ends, but also, through the
Church, to an absolutely supreme end which is supernatural and which is the very end of the Kingdom of
God. Moreover, it is superelevated in its own order.[10]
The natural end of the world—in its threefold character,

[10] I have long insisted on this point—that as a result of the achievements of grace, as a result of grace perfecting nature, nature is
superelevated *in its own order*. In my opinion, the temporal common good of the body politic, for instance, will be superelevated
in a Christian society. Brotherly love, Christian love will play a
part in civil life itself—it is not restricted to the inter-relation between saints in the Kingdom of God. From there it superabounds
and quickens civic friendship. In the same way, I think, philosophy
is superelevated by virtue of its vital relation to theology, from
which it is distinct, of course. To my mind, it is very important
that we admit this superelevation *in the very order of nature*. If we
don't admit it, we are led willy-nilly to a kind of separatism between nature and grace, to a kind of naturalism—nature will have
its own course separately from any contact with grace.

as expressed above—is superelevated by its connection with the supernatural end and with the supernatural virtues. And I would insist that, given the actual condition of the world—that is, the fact that the world is not in a state of pure nature but is vitally and organically related to the Kingdom of God—the *actual* natural end of the world is this natural end superelevated.

But I would also insist again that the natural end of the world, though it is not the absolutely supreme end, is, nevertheless, *a* real end; it is not a mere means. This is a point which is, in my opinion, quite important for the philosopher of history, or of culture in general. In other words, temporal things are not mere means with respect to the attainment of the supernatural end. Of course, they are ordained to it, but not as mere means ordained to an end. I would say that they are intermediate or *infravalent* ends—they are possessed of an intrinsic merit and goodness in themselves, and they are therefore worthy of attainment in themselves, though they are also means with respect to the supernatural end. I am but applying here what St. Thomas says about civil life, to wit, that the common good of civil life is an ultimate end—not the *absolute* ultimate end, but an ultimate end *in a given order*.[11] Similarly, the natural end of the world—in its threefold character—is a *relatively* ultimate end, an ultimate end in the order of nature, whereas only the supernatural end is the *absolutely* ultimate end. It seems to me that there is a serious drawback to disregarding this

[11] See *De virtutibus cardinalibus*, a. 4, ad 3; *Summa theol.*, I-II, 65, 2.

value as end—inferior, infravalent, but still end—of the natural end or ends of the world.[12]

### The mystery of the world

4. I have also indicated in the diagram that, given this superelevation of the world and this relation of the world with the universe of grace, the growth in natural good, as well as, conversely, the growth in evil, are greater now than in the possible case of a world existing in the state of pure nature. At this point we are confronted with what can indeed be called the mystery of the world: not only the mystery involved in the creation itself of nature, but the deeper mystery involved in the commerce between nature and grace, with, on the one hand, the obscure ways (that is, too luminous for our eyes), both exacting and merciful, in which grace penetrates and perfects and transforms nature, and, on the other hand, the tenebrous recesses in which the treacherous and obstinate struggles of nature against grace take place. Natural good and supernatural good are intermingled, and Christ is interested in both. Natural evil and supernatural evil are also intermingled, and the fallen angel is interested in both. He is the Prince of this world.[13]

[12] See also my book, *Neuf leçons sur les notions premières de la philosophie morale* (Paris: Téqui, 1951), pp. 79-81.

[13] Cf. Raïssa Maritain, *Le Prince de ce monde* (Paris: Desclée De Brouwer, 1932); English translation by Dr. G. Phelan, *The Prince of This World* (Toronto: Catholic Extension Press, 1933 and Ditchling, England: St. Dominic's Press, 1936).

The world, however, cannot escape the government of God, the supreme ruler. And Christ and the devil contend with one another for the world,[14] and the world is being snatched by Christ from the devil—not without losses.

In order to sharpen in our minds the sense of this mystery of the world, it is enough to read in the New Testament the passages in which the world is mentioned, and to put them together. Such reading is all the more instructive as it is, at first, puzzling. For in the passages in question the world is spoken of in quite opposite, and seemingly contradictory ways.

Let us quote the most significant of these statements. There are, first, those which can be grouped under the heading: *the World as the Antagonist;* which means, in the first place, and in a most general sense, the Other, the one who is not God (and who has his own ways of life, and who takes part, as was stated above, in the very establishment of the eternal plan). How important does this one appear! Christ was sent to it: "As thou hast sent me into the world, I also have sent them into the world."[15] "Wherefore when he cometh into the world, he saith: *Sacrifice and oblation thou wouldest not: but a body thou hast fitted to me. . . . Then said I: Behold I*

[14] "He that soweth the good seed is the Son of man. And the field is the world. . . . And the enemy that sowed them [the cockle] is the Devil." Matt., 13, 37-39.

[15] John, 17, 18. Cf. ibid., 11, 27; I John, 4, 9.

*come . . .*"[16] And to this one who is not God, God and
Christ must be made known: "*And the world may know
that thou hast sent me and hast loved them, as thou hast
also loved me.*"[17] "*But that the world may know* that I
love the Father: and as the Father hath given me com-
mandments, so do I."[18]

Under the same heading are to be listed, in the second
place, those passages in which the world appears as the
Antagonist in the strict sense of this word—this time as
an enemy and a persecutor, as the one who refuses the
gift of God, nay more, who hates it. ". . . And the world
knew him not."[19] "The world cannot hate you: but me
it hateth."[20] "If the world hate you, know ye that it hath
hated me before you. If you had been of the world, the
world would love its own: but because you are not of
the world, but I have chosen you out of the world, therefore the world hateth you."[21] ". . . And the world hath
hated them: because they are not of the world, as I also
am not of the world. I pray not that thou shouldst take
them out of the world, but that thou shouldst keep them
from evil. They are not of the world, as I also am not
of the world."[22] The Church, like Christ, is from God,
not from the world. And we must choose between being
a friend of the world and a friend of God: "Adulterers,
know you not that the friendship of this world is the
enemy of God?"[23] "Love not the world, nor the things

[16] Hebr., 10, 5-7.      [17] John, 17, 23. (Ital. mine.)
[18] John, 14, 31. (Ital. mine.)      [19] John 1, 10.
[20] John, 7, 7.      [21] John 15, 18-19. Cf. *ibid.*, 8, 23.
[22] John, 17, 14-16.      [23] Epistle of St. James, 4, 4.

which are in the world. If any man love the world, the charity of the Father is not in him. For all that is in the world, is the concupiscence of the flesh and the concupiscence of the eyes and the pride of life, which is not of the Father but is of the world. And the world passeth away and the concupiscence thereof."[24] "By whom the world is crucified to me, and I to the world."[25] The world is in the power of evil: ". . . the whole world is seated in wickedness."[26] "Woe to the world because of scandals".[27] ". . . The prince of this world is already judged."[28] And the world will be condemned: ". . . that we be not condemned with this world."[29] Christ has vanquished the world: ". . . In the world you shall have distress. But have confidence. I have overcome the world."[30]

And then there are those passages which may be grouped under the heading: *the World as redeemed and reconciled* (that is to say, with respect to the merits of Christ, as redeemed by His blood once and for all, and, with respect to the application of these merits, as in the process of being redeemed, throughout history, by the agony of Christ in His mystical body): "For God so loved the world, as to give His only begotten son."[31] That very world, which according to St. Paul will be condemned,[32] God has decided to save through His son: "For God sent not His Son into the world, to judge the

[24] I John 2, 15-17.    [25] Balat., 6, 14.    [26] I John, 5, 19.
[27] Matt., 18, 7.    [28] John, 16, 11.    [29] I Cor., 11, 32.
[30] John, 16, 33. Cf. I John, 5, 4-5.
[31] John, 3, 16.    [32] See *supra*, note 29.

world: but that the world may be saved by him."[33]
". . . for I came not to judge the world, but to save the
world."[34] ". . . Behold the Lamb of God. Behold Him
who taketh away the sin of the world."[35] That very
world, for which He does not pray, He takes away its
sin; He who never knew sin, accepted to be made sin,[36]
and to die, in order to deliver it from its sin.

5. Coming back to our considerations, and our diagram,
let us observe that the world cannot be neutral with
respect to the Kingdom of God. Either it aspires to it
and is quickened by it, or it fights it. In other words, the
relation of the world with the universe of grace is either
a relation of union and inclusion, or a relation of separation and conflict. And here we have the explanation of
the two series of contrasting assertions in the New Testament. If the relation of the world with the Kingdom of
God is a relation of separation and conflict, as indicated
in the diagram of the lower cone by the falling arrow,
then, and to that extent, we have the world as Antagonist
and Enemy to the Kingdom, the world which lies in evil,
the world for which Christ does not pray, the world
which "cannot receive the spirit of truth";[37] and then
come all the statements grouped under the first heading.
If the relation of the world with the Kingdom of God
is a relation of union and inclusion, as indicated by the

[33] John, 3, 17.    [34] John, 12, 47.    [35] John, 1, 29.    [36] II Cor., 5, 21.
[37] "Spiritus veritatis, quem mundus non potest accipere." John, 14, 17.

ascending arrow, then, and to that extent, we have the world as assumed by and in the Kingdom, the world which God loved to the point of giving His only son as a sacrifice, the world whose sin is taken away by the Lamb of God, and for whose salvation the love and sufferings of the Church apply here and now, as long as history lasts, the blood of the Redeemer. And then come all the statements grouped under the second heading.

The apparent antinomy between these two series of statements is thus solved. For the two kinds of relation which I just spoke of, between the world and the Kingdom, take place at the same time. To the extent to which the world separates itself from the Kingdom of God, and goes its own way toward the Prince of this world, we have the first series of statements, the pejorative remarks about the world, finally condemned. To the extent to which the world is permeated with the vital influences of the Kingdom, and embraced and enveloped by it, and carried along by it, we have the statements dealing with the salvation of the world. It is being saved for eternal life, but not as separately taken; it is being saved for eternal life, as taken with the Kingdom and in the Kingdom. And when it will be revealed in its final state of supernatural salvation, this will be beyond time and beyond history—and beyond the present world, beyond *hic mundus:* on the new earth and under the new heavens which will be but one with the Kingdom of God in triumph and glory.

The history of the Church, which is, as Pascal said, the history of the truth, leads as such toward the final revelation of the Kingdom of God—which is something beyond history—and has no other end than that Kingdom completely revealed. But the history of the world is divided between two opposing absolutely ultimate ends —it leads, at one and the same time, toward the kingdom of perdition and toward the Kingdom of God, as termini which are beyond its own natural ends.

And with respect to the relatively ultimate end, the natural end of the world, the same kind of consideration is necessary: this natural end is, as we have seen, three-fold—mastery over nature; conquest of autonomy; and the manifestation of all the potentialities of human nature. But there is an opposite end (in the sense of final result) —the waste and refuse consisting in the accumulation of evil in the course of history. Here we have—in this philosophical perspective—a kind of inferno, of which the world and the history of the world can be freed only if this world ceases to be, only if there is a completely new beginning, a new heaven and a new earth, a transfigured world. Thus we have a kind of philosophical approach to, or preparation for, the theological notion of the transfiguration of the world.

In any case, the absolutely ultimate end, the final end of history is beyond history. For Christian eschatology, there will be a discontinuity between history, which is in time, and the final state of mankind, which will take place in a world transfigured.

I would now propose a further remark on the element of ambivalence that is always to be found in the growth of human history. If we consider historical events, especially big historical events—say, for instance, the Crusades, or the Thirty Years' War, at the time of Richelieu and Father Joseph (Aldous Huxley's mystical theology is questionable but his views on the "Grey Eminence" are of considerable interest for us)[38]—it seems to me that we have to make a distinction between a judgment of *moral* value, relating to the men responsible for such events, and another judgment relating to the *historical* and *cultural* value of the events in question. As to the judgment of moral value, given the examples I have chosen, I would say that the initiative toward the Crusades, both as to the main goal and the secondary political aims, had a highly ethical value (symbolized by the small arrow to the left of the lower figure); whereas the policy of Richelieu and the "Grey Eminence" was Machiavellian and unethical (see small arrow to the right). But if it is a question of the historical or cultural value—not with respect to the men who were responsible for these events, but with respect to the objective significance and impact of the historical actions they brought about—then here we are confronted with the ambivalence of history. No human event is absolutely pure, no human event is absolutely evil—I mean, in the per-

[38] I am thinking of Aldous Huxley's novel *Grey Eminence*, which gives us a challenging, and, I think, tragically true picture of a man who was a real contemplative in the spiritual order and a real Machiavellian in the temporal order.

spective of the cultural and historical value. I would say that the Crusades had for Western civilization salutary effects (symbolized by circle A), but that they were also spoiled by cruelty and a great many impurities, and they had also some harmful implications for Western human history (see corresponding circle below); whereas the Thirty Years' War had historical effects that were surely in the direction of misfortune for Western civilization (see circle B), but at the same time it did produce some really beneficial effects (see corresponding circle above).

## The good of the soul
## and the good of the world

6. I would like to submit further considerations, which deal with human actions—on the one hand, insofar as they have to do with the eternal destiny of man and the inner recesses of his heart, and, on the other hand, insofar as they have to do with the temporal destinies of the world and the impact of man on the history of the world.

With respect to the inner moral life of men, or to the value of their actions and intentions in relation to the absolute ultimate end, in other words, with respect to the hearts of men,[39] I would say first, that the heart of man is either in grace and charity, and directed toward

---

[39] See *Summa theol.,* I-II, 18, 9, where St. Thomas develops the thesis that there are no morally indifferent human actions.

God supremely loved; or it is without grace and charity, and its actions are directed toward a false ultimate end, for instance, self-love. And, secondly, I would but pursue a thesis of Charles Journet[40] when he makes clear how it is that the Church is immaculate, without stain or rust,[41] whereas she is composed of sinners. He holds fast to the thesis that this statement about the immaculate, spotless purity of the Church refers to the Church not only in the future, not only to the glorious Church, but also to the Church in the present life, to the Church here below. He says that the division in question takes place in the heart of each one of us (hence, in my diagram, the figure representing the hearts of men). In the first case, when a man acts in grace and charity, he lives on, he draws life from, the life of the Church—which is a life of grace and charity. It is so because every man who has grace and charity vitally belongs to the Church, either in a visible or in an invisible way. Consequently, the actions in question are not only his, they also manifest in him the very life of the whole a part of which he is. And of course they do not bring any stain to the Church, because they are good, and belong to the Church precisely insofar as they are vivified by the grace of Christ, irrespective of all the minor impurities they may convey. I have indicated all

---

[40] See *L'Eglise du Verbe Incarné*, Vol. II, pp. 1115-1129.
[41] See St. Paul, Ephes., 5, 7. This point was already mentioned *supra*, p. 128.

this on the diagram—when an action emanates from the heart of man in grace and charity, it tends toward the supernatural end, and it belongs to the Kingdom of God itself, to the Church herself.

But in the second case, even if the men in question are visible members of the Church, they withdraw from her life, they slip away from the life of the Church. And the evil actions that they commit are no stain on the Church, on the Kingdom of God, because they are not hers. I have indicated on the diagram that such actions tend toward evil and the Prince of this world.

Thus it is that the divide between the streams which flow from the Church, and those which do not, is to be found in the inner recesses of the hearts of men.

If we consider now no longer the hearts of men, but the external actions they introduce into being, I would suggest that there is a threefold division of these actions (symbolized in my diagram by the circle surrounding the heart). There are actions (section 1) which come from grace and charity, and which directly improve the good of the world. And there are actions (section 2) which come from a heart separated from grace and charity, and which directly increase the amount of evil in the world. These first two categories of actions present no difficulty here. But my point is that there are also actions (section 3) which are good (in the natural order, that is) and which are committed by sinners; they are of no value for eternal life, but they are of value for the world. As indicated in my diagram, such actions can cooperate in one way or another in the increase of good in the world.

St. Thomas holds that a man whose actions are not quickened by grace and charity may have natural virtues in an imperfect state, and be able to do some particular good things, like planting vineyards or building a house.[42] But these particular good things play, it seems to me, a tremendously large part in the history of the world. Take, for instance, the realm of art (and we know how mankind needs art and poetry). How many artists gave masterpieces to the world while being committed to a sinful life! I recall Shelley's saying the sins of the poet are washed away by Time the redeemer. This is not true of the soul of the poet, but it is true of his work, because with the growth of time the work is purified, so to speak, and we can admire it without being wounded by it.

We may make a similar observation with respect to the political achievements of men. Many social and political achievements, which were, as we know, ambivalent, but the main value of which was in the direction

---

[42] St. Thomas writes: "Because human nature is not altogether corrupted by sin, namely, so as to be shorn of every good of nature, even in the state of corrupted nature it can, by virtue of its natural endowments, perform some particular good, such as to build buildings, plant vineyards, and the like; yet it cannot do all the good natural to it, so as to fall short in nothing. In the same way, a sick man can of himself make some movements, yet he cannot be perfectly moved with the movement of one in health, unless by the help of medicine he be cured." *Summa theol.*, I-II, 109, 2.

of the natural good and the progress of the world, were brought about by men who were committed to a sinful life.

It seems to me that we are confronted here with aspects of reality in which the philosophy of history from its own point of view is especially interested. It is more interested in them than is the theology of history because for the theologian, who is mainly concerned with the supernatural end and the Kingdom of God, the category of actions in question must be recognized, of course, but it is not of so deep and great concern as it is for the philosopher.

7. A further point must be made. The relation of the world to the Kingdom of God may be, we have said, either a relation of union and inclusion, or a relation of separation and conflict. Such a distinction deals with things which belong to the realm of morality—first, *qua individual* morality, which essentially relates to the inner life of conscience and expresses itself in the actions of the individual; second, *qua social* morality, which relates to the structures of civilization, and to laws and institutions, and expresses itself in social behavior. At this point it is relevant to observe that since the structures of the social order and of civilization have essentially to do with the *external* relations between men, they, consequently, are fit to receive any formative influence from the Kingdom of God only to the extent to which the

presence of the latter among men is also made externally apparent. This happened more or less in the Gentile world before Christ, but in a merely inchoate way and through some enigmatic prophetic signs (a symbol of which were the "Sibyls" for Christian antiquity and the Middle Ages).[43] So that it may be said that, as long as the message of the Kingdom of God was not publicly revealed and explicitly manifested, externally expressed in our human language, the structures of the social order and of civilization could not receive, save in an exceptional and sporadic manner, the formative influence of the Kingdom; consequently, it was not in and through social morality and the social structures of civilization, but only in and through the conscience and morality of individuals, so far as they invisibly belonged to the Church, and through their personal action on the cultural environment, that any vital connection with, and quickening by, the Kingdom of God could, as a rule, exist for the world. Thus we understand that before the promulgation of the Gospel any human civilization (except that of the Hebrew people) fell within the category of *heathendom*, whose social morality was not inspired by, but rather divided from, the Kingdom. As regards social morality, and the external structures of civilization, the world—even the Indian world with its thirst for deliverance and contemplation, and the Greek world

---

[43] Cf. Charles Journet, *L'Eglise du Verbe Incarné*, Vol. II, pp. 953, 1107-1108.

with its rational wisdom, and the Roman world with its sense of the law and of right—was seated in the shadow of death. After the promulgation of the Gospel a Christendom was possible.[44] A Christendom is a "Christian world." Yet any "world" of Christian denomination, any "Christian world" is not a Christendom; in other terms, the notion of a Christian world includes that of Christendom but is much larger.

Here we have to bring out the notion of "Christian world" in all its generality, and to lay stress on its true significance. This notion is essentially distinct from the notion of Christianity or the notion of the Church. The Christian world is part of this world, it consists—in the various periods of human history—either of those areas of civilization or of those strata in temporal society which are of Christian denomination. But while the areas or strata in question are of Christian denomination, this does not mean that they behave according to Christian standards and inspiration. And the deficiencies of the Christian world, or worlds, are both inevitable and disastrous in the course of human history. Let us only think of those kinds of Christian worlds which were, for instance, the court of Louis XIV in France, or the Prussian Christian State at the time of Friedrich Wilhelm II, or the French upper classes at the time of *le trône et l'autel*, or the English upper classes at the time of the *sweating system*.

Hence it is that our distinction between the world as

[44] On the notion of Christendom, see *infra*, pp. 156 ff.

vitally activated by the Kingdom of God and the world as separating itself from the Kingdom is true not only with respect to *hic mundus* in general, but with respect to the Christian world (or worlds) in particular. These Christian worlds are both vitally inspired by the Kingdom of God in a certain regard and to a certain extent, and, in another regard and to another extent, divided from it by sin. And as far as they are divided from the Kingdom they will bestow their favors upon Christ's disciples in a somewhat strange manner. In the Pagan world of old the Christian was persecuted by being killed, stoned, crucified, thrown to the beasts. In the Christian world the Christian—I mean the man or woman who really lives according to Christian standards and according to the inspiration of the Spirit of God (whose gifts we receive with divine grace, and which are, St. Thomas teaches, necessary for salvation)—is persecuted in another way, less violent but no less real: is there, even, nicer persecution than fraternal persecution? Joan of Arc was burned alive. St. John of the Cross was cast into gaol, St. Theresa of Lisieux was gently and inexorably pushed into the embrace of death. It is in an analogical manner indeed that the statements of the Gospel on the world—insofar as shut up in itself—are to be understood of the Pagan world and of the Christian world. In any case, let us never forget the basic fact that, according to the Gospel, the world will never be fully reconciled with Christ within the course of human history. St. Paul says:

"And all who want to live piously in Christ Jesus shall suffer persecution."[45] This is a universal statement, valid for any period of time. And we find another terrible statement in St. Mark: "And you shall be hated by all men for my name's sake."[46] It's certainly not a very optimistic statement with respect to the world.

The Christian, because he is not of the world, will always be a foreigner in the world—I mean, in the world as separating itself from the Kingdom of God and shutting itself up in itself; he is incomprehensible to the world and inspires it with uneasiness and distrust. The world cannot make sense of the theological virtues. Theological faith, the world sees as a challenge, an insult, and a threat; it is by reason of their faith that it dislikes Christians, it is through their faith that they vanquish it; faith is enough to divide them from the world. Theological hope, the world does not see at all; it is simply blind to it. Theological charity, the world sees the wrong way; it misapprehends it, is mistaken about it. It confuses it with any kind of quixotic devotion to whatever human cause it may profit by. And thus does the world tolerate charity, even admire it—insofar as it is not charity, but something else. (And so is charity the secret weapon of Christianity.)

In the last analysis, it is exceedingly hard for the world to acknowledge the fact that the Christian may simply be; it cannot make room for the existence of the Chris-

[45] II Tim., 3, 12.    [46] Mark, 13, 13.

tian, except by virtue of some misunderstanding. If we really were what we are, and if the world knew us as we are, how pleased it would be to recognize it as its sacred obligation to mow us down, in self-defense. . . .

And yet, let us never forget, on the other hand, that the world, treacherous as it may be, is (insofar as it is open to, and assumed by, the Kingdom of God) redeemed and quickened by the blood of Christ, and that it badly needs to have Christians—who are not of it— live and work and love and suffer in it, in order for it to advance toward its ends.

This great need of the world is true, first, with respect to the natural ends of the world—modern history appears in this regard as revealing more and more, at each step, how necessary the temporal mission of the Christian is. Here we have an outstanding instance of the historical law of progressive *prise de conscience*.

And this great need of the world is still truer (it's a very datum of Christian revelation) with respect to the final supernatural end of the world, and to the meta-historic fulfillment of mankind's salvation. For there is, as I remarked previously, a continued work of redemption accomplished in the Mystical Body and to which all men of good will indirectly contribute in the order of dispositive causality, but which in the very order of instrumental efficient causality is brought about by the active members of Christ, i.e., the baptized who live in grace—in short, by the application of the merits of Christ

all along the course of time. Thus it is that the persecuted and the saints, who are saved by Christ, save as
instrumental causes, and by virtue of the blood of Christ,
the persecutors and the evildoers. Poor persecutors and
poor sinners, poor prodigal sons who are struggling in
the experience of evil and the unholy business of the
world, will thus be saved, except those who have killed
within themselves any divine seed of good will and who
prefer Hell to God. With the exception of these men
who refuse to be redeemed, that very world which hates
Christ and His disciples will be finally reconciled to
Christ, but after the end of history. Here we have an
application of that law mentioned by St. Paul, of which
we spoke in the previous chapter—God has imprisoned
all things under sin in order to have mercy on all.

## Thy Kingdom come

*8.* In one sense, the Kingdom of God has already come
—in the form of the Church, or the Mystical body of
Christ, which is, as we have seen, the Kingdom in the
state of pilgrimage and crucifixion. In another sense, the
Kingdom of God is to come, namely, as to its fulfillment
in the Jerusalem of glory—the Church triumphant—and
in the world of the resurrection. It is in relation to this
second sense that we have to consider the problem of the
Kingdom of God on earth, or of the realization of the
Gospel on earth. To my mind, there are three kinds of

error in this matter. There is the *anthropocratic* illusion, according to which man himself and man alone—that is to say, either the power of science and human reason, or the self-movement of human history—is in charge of bringing about the Kingdom of God here below. There is the *satanocratic* illusion, according to which the world is completely abandoned to the Devil, with no kind of veritable progress and of realization of the Gospel, imperfect as it may be, to be hoped for in our social-temporal and political order—a view that is not without some impact in the Protestant world,[47] and also in the Greek Orthodox world. And there is the *theocratic* illusion, which would make the world—*hic mundus*, our historical world, and the social-temporal and political City—into the Kingdom of God.

This problem is a most important one, not only theoretically but practically. To bring things closer to our imagination, allow me to recall that it was forcefully posed a few years ago by the Austrian playwright Hochwälder, in a play produced in Paris with considerable success,[48] entitled *Sur la terre comme au ciel*.[49] The author, though not a Christian himself, found the matter for a veritable, I think, Christian tragedy in the social achievements of the Spanish Jesuits in Paraguay, and in the final catastrophe of this great venture. The Jesuits

[47] See above, Chapter II, pp. 49-50.
[48] In New York it was a failure.
[49] Paris: Table Ronde, 1952. [*Das heilige Experiment.*]

were able to start a kind of perfect socio-political establishment, where the Indian workers were justly treated
in every respect. It was a paternalistic society, but a really
Christian paternalistic society. Everybody was happy,
and many conversions took place. At the moment when
the play opens (this is but a scanty summary), the Provincial of the Jesuits, who is not only a religious superior but
also a temporal administrator (he is the head of this
Jesuit settlement), is quite pleased with the results, and
he thanks God for them. But then a high official of the
Spanish court, sent by the King, arrives and tells the
Provincial that these things must cease because they are
greatly disturbing the Spanish colonists around—the
Jesuits had established a kind of State within a State, and
the other State, the Spanish colony, was lacking in man-
power (everybody was going to the Jesuit establishment), and was being torn by much social unrest and a
great deal of resentment. However, the high official is
finally taken prisoner by the Jesuit Provincial.

But then a representative of the Jesuit General arrives
from Rome, and orders the Provincial to abandon the
whole undertaking. And despite great resistance on the
part of the people, the Provincial realizes that he must
obey—and not only because of blind obedience, but
also (as he indicates in a quite interesting discussion with
the representative of the General) because he now sees
that there was something wrong with the whole endeavor. The Jesuits were primarily interested in a job

which was not their primary job; instead of dedicating their energies primarily and above all to their priestly mission, to the preaching of the Gospel and the expansion of the realm of grace, they were, in actual existence (even if in their intention the spiritual goal came first) dedicated to realizing a temporal task, trying to achieve the Kingdom of God on earth in a temporal way. Indeed when the Provincial asked the Indians why they had come to the Jesuits, and why they had become converted, they replied that it was not because of the love of God, but rather because they wanted a happy and just life on earth. And so the play ends with the heart-rending ruin—which was historically true—of the Jesuit establishment, and with this ruin fully accepted by the Jesuit Provincial, who is wounded while stopping a riot and pays for the whole venture with his own life.

Now the author was not interested, of course, in giving us any answer. And also, we may remark, he exaggerates the opposition. On the one hand, the representative of the Jesuit General seems to affirm in the discussion that we must be fully resigned to injustice here below. Though more implicit than explicit, his is the *satanocratic* conception—the world is abandoned to evil and injustice. On the other hand, the Jesuit Provincial tries to establish a Kingdom of God here below, and even (at least before the end of the play) allows, however involuntarily, this temporal achievement to take precedence over the preaching of the supratemporal Kingdom. His is the *theocratic* conception. At any rate, the play aroused much discussion, largely because it offers no solution. Some people were horrified by it, and some others quite pleased.

But what is the truth of the matter? In my opinion, it is that we must seek with all our power a genuine (I mean actual and vital, not only decorative), imperfect as it may be, realization in this world of the requirements of the Gospel. The fact of so many millions of men starving and living in despair, in a life unworthy of man, is an insult to Christ and to brotherly love. As a result, the temporal mission of the Christian is to strive to eradicate such evils, and to build up a Christian-inspired social and political order, where justice and brotherhood are better and better served. Yet this job is primarily the job of the Christian laity, working in the very midst of the world and civilization; it is not primarily the job of the Christian priesthood (and it is especially not their job to found, as the Jesuits did in Paraguay, a temporal establishment divided from the temporal community as a whole). Furthermore, there is a hierarchy of ends, and the Word of God comes first; it is imperative progressively to transform terrestrial life according to the requirements of natural law and of the Gospel; nevertheless, the absolutely ultimate goal is not to transform terrestrial life, but to have souls enter eternal life and finally the vision of God; and the "horizontal" effort itself, directed to transforming the world, essentially needs, in the depths of human history, the "vertical" effort directed to expanding the realm of grace in souls; for both efforts are, in the long run, necessary to one another; but the most necessary is the vertical one. Thus, there will always be a clash between a Christian and an atheist with respect to the work to be achieved here on earth because in doing this work the atheist pursues his absolutely ultimate end, the Christian pursues his ultimate end in a certain order only (*finis ultimus secundum quid*), dependent as it is on an absolutely ultimate end which is supratemporal. The realization of the Gospel in temporal life that Christians must hope for and strive for will always be, in one way or another, deficient and thwarted; this world will never be fully reconciled with Christ within history. We will never have the Kingdom of God within temporal history. This is all the more reason why we should strive toward it. But we know that it will never come about before the end of history. There can be no rest for the Christian as long as justice and love do not hold sway over the lives of men. And since their requirements will never be completely fulfilled within history, the Christian will therefore never have rest within history—and that's perfectly proper to his condition. . . .

*9. Thy Kingdom come:* when Christians say every day to God these words of the Lord's prayer, what are they requesting, and willing, with respect to the Kingdom in

the state of fulfillment? They want, they will the Kingdom of God to come together with the resurrection of
the dead, beyond history. And they want, they will—
on earth, in this world, within history—the unceasing
*march* toward the Kingdom of God. The Kingdom in
its full completion will only come after the end of time;
but the actual march toward the Kingdom, at each step
of history, is a thing which can be, and should be, carried
into effect on earth, in this world, within history. And
for this march toward the Kingdom Christians must not
only pray, they also must indefatigably work and strive.

In such a perspective the notion of Christendom takes
on its full meaning and full dimensions. The notion of
Christendom is clearly distinct from the notion of Christianity, and from that of the Church. Christendom means
a Christian-inspired civilization—not a simply decorative
Christian world, but a really and vitally Christian-inspired civilization. Christendom pertains to the temporal
realm, it pertains to the world, to the world as superelevated in its own natural order by the Christian leaven.
If there is, as I believe, a temporal mission for the Christian, how would it be possible for the terrestrial hope by
which such a mission is quickened not to have as its most
comprehensive aim the ideal of building either a better
or a new Christian civilization? The will, and dream,
of a Christendom to be established or to be improved
is the will and dream of Christians laboring in the world.
There was a real and genuine (though imperfect, and

spoiled with many stains) Christendom in the Middle Ages. At each new age in human history (as is, to my mind, our own age with respect to the Middle Ages and the Baroque Age), it is normal that Christians hope for a new Christendom, and depict for themselves, in order to guide their effort, a concrete historical ideal appropriate to the particular climate of the age in question.

In any Christendom, old or new, evil and the devil will, no doubt, have their part; as I have just said, Christendom belongs to the realm of the world. Yet, because it is a Christian world in a particularly genuine and eminent sense, in other words, because it is a world actually and vitally Christian-inspired in its very structures and institutions, the part of God and the part of the good is decisively prevalent in it and stirs it forward, as long as it does not start to fall into decadence. During the centuries in which a Christendom develops and grows, the world advances more rapidly toward its natural ends (superelevated in their own order, as we have seen) and toward the meta-historical Kingdom of God. Its march toward the Kingdom is accelerated.

A Christendom, in which the march of mankind toward the Kingdom of God is thus accelerated, implies in actual fact a certain realization of the Gospel good tidings on earth. Nevertheless the fact remains that in it, because it is part of the world, "all those who want to live piously in Christ Jesus" will continue to "suffer persecution." This is in no way surprising. It is but a particular application of a general law of temporal history. The main advances in human history—insofar as they are not merely technical, but morally directed toward the common good of mankind and a state of affairs more fitted to the dignity of man—are acquired at the price not only of blood and sweat, but of much love and self-sacrifice also. Yet, once the change in question has been obtained through the effort of a few men and the agony of the spirit in them, it becomes either institutionalized or integrated in the collective consciousness—in any case absorbed in the very fabric of this world, which is thus carried to a higher level of human civilization but which still remains the world where both God and the devil have their parts. It is the same with Christendom. It lives on the unceasing gift of themselves that the best of its members make to the common good; but every triumph of such human devotion and spiritual energy, while it raises the history of the world to a higher level, at the same time is absorbed and integrated in the temporal fabric of the world, whose institutions and agencies, laws and common consciousness, social life and general behavior are made more consonant with the requirements of the Gospel, but which still remains the world where saints will never be short of persecution.

But let us turn now toward another aspect of the question, and, once again, toward the relation between the world and the Kingdom of God no longer considered in the state of fulfillment, but in the state of pilgrimage and crucifixion, the Kingdom of God as already come among us, in other words the Church or the mystical body of Christ. Obviously, nowhere in human history do the promptings of the Kingdom play a greater part than in the periods when a Christian-inspired civilization, a Christendom develops. Furthermore, it is normal that the mystical body of Christ should act on the world with the full energy of the divine life whose communication to human souls is maintained in a state of unscathed integrity by the undiminished teaching of revealed truth, the plenitude of the sacraments and the ties of undamaged discipline. Yet it may happen that, under given historical circumstances, the temporal structures of civilization find themselves more open to the influence of the mystical body in certain areas where its divine energy is, by reason of religious division, in a more or less impoverished state, but where its impact on temporal society meets with lesser obstacles caused either by too long inertia, in a number of Christians, with respect to their temporal mission, or by a hardening against religion in a number of unbelievers.[50] As a result, it is possible that, at a given time, the area in the world

[50] Then it is relevant to say, as I put it in another book, that Catholicism "rejoices, without envy, in every good even though it be achieved outside its boundaries—for that good is outside Catholic boundaries only in semblance; in reality it belongs to it invisibly" (*Religion et Culture*, 2nd ed., Paris, Desclée De Brouwer, 1946, p. 62). And so the proper task of Catholics is to recognize such a good, and to further it, and to improve it if possible.

in which a Christian-inspired civilization has a chance of finding an appropriate soil for future development may happen to be an area where the promptings of the mystical body of Christ on temporal life pass, for a large part, through men of good will who belong to it invisibly,[51] and where its visible forces do not play the major part in the common inspiration. Such is, in my opinion, the case with this country at the present epoch. The Catholic Church plays a growing part in American life, and I think that American Catholics are called to

[51] As a matter of fact we see that in modern times many badly needed achievements in the temporal order which were Christian-inspired— one thinks, for instance, of the final abolition of slavery (*Uncle Tom's Cabin*), the improvement in the penitentiary system, assistance to victims of war (The Red Cross), the prohibition of legalized prostitution, the struggle against alcoholism—came from Protestant initiatives. The humanitarian activity of the Quakers is a great testimony to Christian inspiration. Cf. Charles Journet, *Exigences chrétiennes en politique* (Paris: Egloff, 1945), pp. 438-448, apropos of Max Huber's *Le bon Samaritain, considérations sur l'Evangile et le travail de la Croix-Rouge* (Neuchâtel, 1943).

As regards the American Constitution, I observed in another book: "Paradoxically enough, and by virtue of the serious religious feelings of the Founding Fathers, it appeared, at a moment of unstable equilibrium (as all moments in time are) in the history of ideas, as a lay—even, to some extent, rationalist—fruit of the perennial Christian life-force, which despite three centuries of tragic vicissitudes and spiritual division was able to produce this momentous temporal achievement at the dawn of the American nation: as if the losses suffered by human history in the supreme domain of the integrity and unity of faith, and in the interest in theological truth, had been the price paid, with respect to human weakness and entanglements, for the release at that given moment of humbler, temporal Christian energies that must at any cost penetrate the historical existence of mankind." (*Man and the State*, The University of Chicago Press, p. 183.)

a particularly important historic role, if they fully understand their mission, especially their intellectual mission, in cooperating in the forward movement of the national community as a whole. Yet the fact remains that in its historical roots, and in the cast of mind of its Founding Fathers, as well as in the moral structure of its secular consciousness, America is more of a Protestant than a Catholic country. The religious tradition of America appears more and more as a threefold religious tradition: Protestant, Catholic and Jew.[52] And, as a matter of fact, America is today the area in the world in which, despite powerful opposite forces and currents, the notion of a Christian-inspired civilization is more part of the national heritage than in any other spot on earth. If there is any hope for the sprouting of a new Christendom in the modern world, it is in America that the historical and ethico-social ground which could become a soil for such a sprouting may be found[53]—assuming, as we do, that the opposing trends toward secularism no. 1 (national life cut off from religion) or secularism no. 2 (religion made subservient to national progress), toward anti-liberal conformism or toward utopian technocratism, are overcome.

My last remark has to do with the fact that in the Christian perspective—precisely because the Kingdom of

[52] Cf. Will Herberg, *Protestant, Catholic, Jew* (New York: Doubleday, 1955.)
[53] See my book *Reflections on America* (New York: Scribners, 1958), Ch. XIX.

God as fully accomplished will come *after* the end of history—the march of the world toward the Kingdom, and its progress toward its natural ends (together with the simultaneous progress toward evil) will unceasingly be in the making and unceasingly go on as long as history lasts. Here appears a basic difference between the Christian philosophy of history and the Hegelian, Marxian or Comtian philosophies of history. Be they dialectical or positivist, these philosophies of pure immanentist or atheist evolution are inevitably bound to a patent self-contradiction. On the one hand, they insist that Becoming is the only reality, and the process of change continues without end; and, on the other hand, they offer themselves as the definitive and final revelation, at the end of time, of the meaning of all history. The Christian philosophy of history is not liable to such inconsistencies. The end is beyond time, and never therefore can the movement of history come to a definitive and final state, or a definitive and final self-revelation, within time. Never can a Christian philosopher of history install himself, as Hegel, Marx and Comte did, at the end of time.

And never can Christians rest within time. As long as the world exists, the Christian must always search for new progress and new improvement, for more justice and brotherhood on earth, and for a deeper and more complete realization of the Gospel here below. For him there can never be enough. It is always imperative to *do more.* Just as Christians must unceasingly strive, each in his own individual life, for the eternal salvation of his soul and of the world, so they must, in the succession of centuries, unceasingly strive to foster and fulfil, better and better, in this world, men's terrestrial hope in the Gospel.

## Chapter 5

# FINAL REMARKS

### Philosophy and History

*1.* The main intention of this book was to stress the possibility, and the validity, of certain philosophical laws —either functional or vectorial—which enlighten human history and make it more intelligible to us, but which neither *explain* it nor subject the course of historical events to *necessity;* these events are necessary with respect only to general features and patterns within which it is up to human freedom to determine the particular orientation which gives them typically human significance. It was on purpose, moreover, that I limited myself to a number of more or less disconnected instances and of partial (though, in my opinion, basic) insights in the field of the philosophy of history. I wanted to emphasize the modesty of the task, and the necessity of avoiding any hasty systematization.

I was, thus, very much concerned with the critical or gnoseological aspects of the problem. In order to make my positions clearer on that score, I should like to pick up, for a brief discussion, Professor John U. Nef's book, *War and Human Progress.*

Werner Sombart had insisted that war, and the tensions engendered by war, are historical factors which foster human progress. Such a statement, the Hegelian background of which was clear enough, dealt with a problem typically pertaining to the philosophy of history, and offered us a particular law (functional law) in this domain. Now John Nef undertook to verify this so-called law against the background of historical facts. And on the basis of an extremely large and detailed body of information, and a most careful analysis dealing with our post-mediaeval centuries, he came to the conclusion that Sombart's assumption was wrong. The law stated by him is belied by the facts. Here, thus, we have a case in which history disproves an erroneous philosophy of history. Yet, by the same stroke, the historical work in question proves to concern itself with notions—such as human progress and the scale of values involved—which pertain to the realm of the philosophy of history. Let us say that in a book like Professor Nef's what we are dealing with is "history philosophically oriented" or "history integrally taken." In order to have philosophy of history properly speaking, the philosophical notions to which I just alluded should be explicitly brought out, and discussed for their own sake. We would have to look for a philosophical definition of human progress, and for a philosophical definition of war, and for the reasons, drawn from the nature of things, which enlighten and steady the inductive inference that war is not by itself a factor of human progress; we would have to extend our analysis to other civilizations, and also to primitive societies, to the anthropological distinction and relationship between hunting and warlike activities, etc.

To have a complete picture of the mutual connections between philosophy and history, let us point out, then, that *moral philosophy* is at the most abstract and universal level, and *merely factual history* at the most concrete level in the picture.

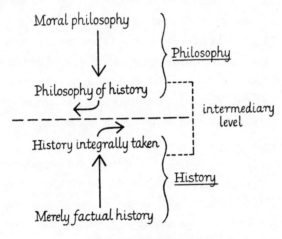

DIAGRAM NUMBER 4

The intermediary level is that at which philosophy and history meet, all the while remaining distinct in nature from one another. Here a distinction must be made. On the one hand, we have *history integrally taken,* in which the historian moves up, so to speak, from the level of merely factual history toward philosophy—without, for all that, reaching the level of philosophy proper. And, on the other hand, we have the *philosophy of history*, in which the philosopher moves down from the level of moral philosophy toward history, without, for all that, reaching the level of history proper.

At this point, if we remember what was said in our first chapter about historical knowledge, we shall perceive that history integrally taken is real, full-fledged, or grown-up history—that very history whose truth depends on the trustworthiness or multifarious truth-value of the whole intellectual fabric of the historian, and of his philosophy of man and of life.[1] Let me note, in this connection, and this is quite significant, that the revival of the classical, humanistic idea of history which we are contemplating today brings real history to the fore anew.

Merely factual history is of the utmost necessity. But it is not a "science," as the naïve positivism of the nineteenth century fancied. It is an integral part of history, as an indispensable technique and discipline (critique of documents, critique of testimonies, paleography, etc.) aiming to "observe" past occurrences and to prepare an accurately sifted body of material which the historian will have to weigh, evaluate, and articulate

[1] See *supra*, chapter I, pp. 6-8, and especially the passages from H. Marrou quoted in Footnotes 6 and 8, p. 8.

for a correct understanding of the sequence of events in their individual or singular interdependence.

It is not by trying in vain to make itself into a pseudo-science; it is by integrating itself with a true system of human, moral and cultural values, in other words, by orienting itself toward philosophy, or by philosophically maturing, that history reaches its full typical dimensions *qua* history, and is real history. So it is that nowhere does the moral philosopher profit by a richer supply of diffused, unsystematized human wisdom (*in actu exercito*) than in the reading of great historians. Furthermore, it is normal for the historian—the real historian—to have a yearning for, and a leaning toward, the philosophy of history, as it is normal for the physicist or the biologist to have a yearning for, and a leaning toward, the philosophy of nature. Yet, in both cases the line of demarcation can be safely crossed, and the yearning in question genuinely satisfied, only if one really becomes a philosopher, in other words, if one really becomes equipped with a new intellectual virtue. Let it be added, incidentally, that, taken in itself, and whatever practical lessons may be drawn from it, history, which belongs by nature to the narrative genre, essentially pertains to the speculative or theoretical order; whereas the philosophy of history, which is part of moral philosophy, pertains to the order of practical (speculativo-practical) wisdom.

### Philosophy of History
### and supra-philosophical data

2. In the preceding chapter I spoke a great deal of the Church, the Kingdom of God, and the supernatural order. I had to do so in order to deal with my own specific problem—the problem of the world. There is a mystery of the world, utterly different from, and closely connected with, the mystery of the Church. And my point is that if a genuine and adequately taken philosophy of history is to develop, both theologians and philosophers will have to establish as a basis for it an articulate notion of that kind of mystery which is designated by this strange and ambiguous word, "the world." A very strange word—meaning at the same time the cosmos of Greek philosophy and the *hic mundus* of the Gospel—and one that must be examined and sifted!

Also, a certain number of the examples I gave throughout the book had to do with that connection between philosophy and theological data which is, in my opinion, a characteristic of moral philosophy adequately taken. In other words, the aspect "Christian philosophy of history" was especially stressed in my notion of the philosophy of history. The reason for this is twofold. On the one hand, as I have remarked many times, there is no complete or adequate philosophy of history if it is not connected with some prophetic or theological data. On the other hand (and this is something contingent and accidental), my own reflections and remarks on the philosophy of history were, in fact, prompted for many years by the practical problem of the plight of Christians in contemporary society—their temporal difficulties and temporal responsibilities—and by an effort to discover and elaborate an intellectual equipment that could answer this problem. As a result, I was led to pay special attention to the supra-philosophical data with which philosophy must deal from its own point of view in the philosophy of history. If I had ever undertaken a systematic work in the philosophy of history, I would have had to embark on a larger and more detailed study of the merely natural aspects of the philosophy of history, especially as concerns the comparative study of civilizations.

3. Now if we look for a completely non-theological or a merely rational and natural approach in the philosophy of history, we may think of the work of Toynbee, for instance, though Toynbee, in my opinion, is more a historian passionately fond of philosophical generalizations, than a philosopher. He also seems to be very fond of drawing or squeezing from history a sort of theology of his own: but this in no way means that he is interested in enlightening his philosophy of history with any verity provided by theology. For all that, his *A Study of History*, essentially concerned with the birth and dissolution of civilizations, pertains by nature to the philosophy of history. And it is a good example of an honest and

fair attempt in the philosophy of history, as opposed to the work of Spengler, for instance, who, to my mind, was a rather questionable wisdom-monger.

We find in Toynbee's work examples of what I have called typological formulas or vectorial laws, as when he characterizes a civilization in its typical dynamism, e.g., the civilization of the Osmanlis, or that of the Spartans. And we also find a great number of axiomatic formulas or functional laws, as when he tries to bring out the universal laws to which every civilization is subjected —say, such a law as what he calls "the challenge of the environment." As he puts it, "the greater the challenge, the greater the stimulus"; "the interaction of challenge and response is subject to a law of diminishing returns"; "there is a *mean range* of severity at which the stimulus is at its highest, and we will call this degree the optimum, as contrasted with the maximum." And when he speaks of the failure of self-determination, with the three forms of the nemesis of creativity: idolization of an ephemeral self, idolization of an ephemeral institution, or idolization of an ephemeral technique; or with the suicidalness of militarism; or with intoxication with victory—all that is philosophical generalization stating kinds of axiomatic laws. And all that, I dare say, provides us with rather scanty intellectual food, and teaches us scarcely more than plain common sense could teach us. Strangely enough, Toynbee seems to be much more concerned with these axiomatic or functional laws—which, given his merely comparative method, cannot help appearing at times as common-sense truisms or somewhat platitudinous generalities—than with typological or vectorial laws.[2]

So it is that Toynbee's remarkable, immensely erudite and thoroughly conscientious work is finally disappointing. It misses the mark because it is too ambitious (it claims to explain history) and insufficiently equipped (it is not integrated in a general philosophy); and, above all, because it resides in a sphere entirely extraneous to moral philosophy adequately taken. Toynbee discards the possibility of having his rational inquiry assisted and complemented by any theological light and prophetic data. Hence the shallowness to which I alluded. When it comes to Christianity, for instance, its development is historically explicable, in Toynbee's opinion, in the same way as that of "Mithraism and its other rivals in the Hellenic world," and nearly all the "higher religions,"

[2] Contrariwise, these typological laws occupy a larger place in the work of John Nef and his effort to characterize, in the whole complexity of their elements, the various epochs in modern history, especially the Industrial Age. See John Nef, *La naissance de la civilisation industrielle et le monde contemporain* (Paris: Librairie Armand Colin, 1954).

I can only briefly mention here Professor David B. Richardson's article "The Philosophy of History and the Stability of Civilizations," in *The Thomist*, April, 1957, which I read while correcting my proofs. For the author of this excellent essay, the philosophy of history is, as it is for me, part of ethical philosophy—and of a Christian ethical philosophy. I was particularly interested in his analysis of historical cycles, in which he suggests a philosophical interpretation of Toynbee's observations about the growth and decline of civilizations.

that is, as an effect of the reactions of an internal proletariat which feels itself *in* but not *of* the society, and
which receives its inspiration from a spring that gushed
forth in some alien civilization. Such analogies have, no
doubt, an interest in the field of material causality, but
by way of an "explanation" they are strictly nothing.

Christopher Dawson has given us an excellent criticism of Toynbee in an article in *The Commonweal*.[3]
Apropos of the final four volumes of *A Study of History*,
he observes that "Toynbee introduces the new principle
which marks a fundamental modification of his earlier
views and involves the transformation of his *Study of
History* from a relativist phenomenology of equivalent
cultures, after the fashion of Spengler, to a unitary
philosophy of history comparable to that of the idealist
philosophers of the nineteenth century. This change,
which was already foreshadowed in the fifth volume,
means the abandonment of Toynbee's original theory of
the philosophical equivalence of the civilzations and the
introduction of a qualitative principle embodied in the
Higher Religions, regarded as representatives of a higher
species of society, which stand in the same relation to
the civilizations as the latter to the primitive societies."
Toynbee ceases to admit the philosophical equivalence
of the civilizations, but it is in order to admit now the
theological equivalence of what he calls the "Higher

[3] "Toynbee's Odyssey of the West," *The Commonweal*, LXI, No. 3
(Oct. 22, 1954), pp. 62-67. See also H. Marrou, *op. cit.*, pp. 202-203.

Religions," i.e., Mahayana Buddhism, Christianity, Islam, and Hinduism.

Moreover, in Toynbee's perspective, civilization is oriented toward religion and quickened by it, but at the same time the final aim and *raison d'être* of religion is to provide for the spiritual unity of mankind. And for him "the real problem of the future," to quote Dawson again, "is whether the four Religions will realize their mission by uniting mankind in a four-part spiritual symphony or whether their mutual antagonisms and intolerance will lead to the loss of their mandate and their supercession by a new world religion of the Secondary type," i.e., by one of the approximately dozen modern, or not so modern, religious movements, such as Sikhism, Bedreddinism, etc. A rather silly prophecy from an author who has never looked for genuine prophetic data there where they can be found.

The only light that Toynbee gives us about the final direction of human history is the necessity, which I just mentioned, for spiritual unification. Well, how does he know that it is imperative for mankind to achieve spiritual unity on earth? This can be considered a questionable assumption, founded on considerations as gratuitous and *a priori* as those which prevailed in the mind of Auguste Comte. The fact that mankind naturally tends toward more and more complete unity is not a proof that it will, and must, attain complete unity within history. Furthermore, though Toynbee sees civilization, at least in its higher forms, as receiving its meaning from religion and as oriented toward religion, still he finally conceives religion as itself subservient to civilization, because for him the mission of religion is not defined with respect to God and divine truth, but rather with respect to mankind and to the highest level, the spiritual level, of civilization itself. If mankind's unity—to be achieved in this world—were the essential and primary aim of religion (in other words, if Man himself were the supreme end of Religion), God should be considered, as Comte put it, "irreligious," for His Word has brought the sword on earth.[4] It has been said that the Gospel will be preached everywhere; it has not been said that it will be everywhere accepted. We hope, of course, that it will at last be—I mean, within history—but this can only occur through a miracle of grace, not a necessity of nature.

[4] "Think not that I came to send peace on the earth: I came not to send peace, but a sword. For I came to set a man at variance against his father, and the daughter against the mother, and the daughter-in-law against her mother-in-law: And a man's foes shall be they of his own household." Matt., 10, 34-36.

# INDEX OF PROPER NAMES

# Index of Proper Names

179